# MAX LUCADO

## LIFE LESSONS *from*

# EPHESIANS

*Where You Belong*

PREPARED BY THE LIVINGSTONE CORPORATION

THOMAS NELSON
*Since 1798*

Published in Nashville, Tennessee, by Thomas Nelson. Thomas Nelson is a registered trademark of HarperCollins Christian Publishing, Inc.

Produced with the assistance of the Livingstone Corporation. Project staff include Jake Barton, Joel Bartlett, Andy Culbertson, Mary Horner Collins, Will Reaves, and Will Reaves.

Editor: Neil Wilson

All Scripture quotations, unless otherwise indicated, are taken from The Holy Bible, New International Version®, NIV®. Copyright © 1973, 1978, 1984, 2011 by Biblica, Inc.™ Used by permission. All rights reserved worldwide.

Scripture quotations marked MSG are taken from The Message. Copyright © 1993, 1994, 1995, 1996, 2000, 2001, 2002. Used by permission of NavPress Publishing Group.

Scripture quotations marked NCV are taken from the New Century Version®. Copyright © 2005 by Thomas Nelson. Used by permission. All rights reserved.

Scripture quotations marked NKJV are taken from the New King James Version®. Copyright © 1982 by Thomas Nelson. Used by permission. All rights reserved.

Material for the "Inspiration" sections taken from the following books:

*3:16: The Numbers of Hope.* © 2007 by Max Lucado. Thomas Nelson, a registered trademark of HarperCollins Christian Publishing, Inc., Nashville, Tennessee.

*Come Thirsty.* © 2004 by Max Lucado. Thomas Nelson, a registered trademark of HarperCollins Christian Publishing, Inc., Nashville, Tennessee.

*The Gift of the Blessing.* © 1993 by Gary Smalley and John Trent. Thomas Nelson, a registered trademark of HarperCollins Christian Publishing, Inc., Nashville, Tennessee.

*God Came Near.* © 2004 by Max Lucado. Thomas Nelson, a registered trademark of HarperCollins Christian Publishing, Inc., Nashville, Tennessee.

*Grace.* © 2012 by Max Lucado. Thomas Nelson, a registered trademark of HarperCollins Christian Publishing, Inc., Nashville, Tennessee.

*The Great House of God.* © 1997 by Max Lucado. Thomas Nelson, a registered trademark of HarperCollins Christian Publishing, Inc., Nashville, Tennessee.

*He Still Moves Stones.* © 1993 by Max Lucado. Thomas Nelson, a registered trademark of HarperCollins Christian Publishing, Inc., Nashville, Tennessee.

*A Love Worth Giving.* © 2002 by Max Lucado. Thomas Nelson, a registered trademark of HarperCollins Christian Publishing, Inc., Nashville, Tennessee.

*Max on Life.* © 2010 by Max Lucado. Thomas Nelson, a registered trademark of HarperCollins Christian Publishing, Inc., Nashville, Tennessee.

*Next Door Savior.* © 2003 by Max Lucado. Thomas Nelson, a registered trademark of HarperCollins Christian Publishing, Inc., Nashville, Tennessee.

*No Wonder They Call Him the Savior.* © 1986 by Max Lucado. Thomas Nelson, a registered trademark of HarperCollins Christian Publishing, Inc., Nashville, Tennessee.

*Shaped by God* (previously published as *On the Anvil*). © 2001 by Max Lucado. Tyndale House Publishers, Carol Stream, Illinois.

Thomas Nelson titles may be purchased in bulk for educational, business, fundraising, or sales promotional use. For information, please e-mail SpecialMarkets@ThomasNelson.com.

ISBN 978-0-310-08648-2

**First Printing May 2018 / Printed in the United States of America**

# CONTENTS

# CONTENTS

# HOW TO STUDY THE BIBLE

The Bible is a peculiar book. Words crafted in another language. Deeds done in a distant era. Events recorded in a far-off land. Counsel offered to a foreign people. It is a peculiar book.

It's surprising that anyone reads it. It's too old. Some of its writings date back 5,000 years. It's too bizarre. The book speaks of incredible floods, fires, earthquakes, and people with supernatural abilities. It's too radical. The Bible calls for undying devotion to a carpenter who called himself God's Son.

Logic says this book shouldn't survive. Too old, too bizarre, too radical.

The Bible has been banned, burned, scoffed, and ridiculed. Scholars have mocked it as foolish. Kings have branded it as illegal. A thousand times over the grave has been dug and the dirge has begun, but somehow the Bible never stays in the grave. Not only has it survived, but it has also thrived. It is the single most popular book in all of history. It has been the bestselling book in the world for years!

There is no way on earth to explain it. Which perhaps is the only explanation. For the Bible's durability is not found on *earth* but in *heaven*. The millions who have tested its claims and claimed its promises know there is but one answer: the Bible is God's book and God's voice.

As you read it, you would be wise to give some thought to two questions: *What is the purpose of the Bible?* and *How do I study the Bible?* Time spent reflecting on these two issues will greatly enhance your Bible study.

What is the purpose of the Bible?

Let the Bible itself answer that question: *"From infancy you have known the Holy Scriptures, which are able to make you wise for salvation through faith in Christ Jesus"* (2 Timothy 3:15).

The purpose of the Bible? Salvation. God's highest passion is to get his children home. His book, the Bible, describes his plan of salvation. The purpose of the Bible is to proclaim God's plan and passion to save his children.

This is the reason why this book has endured through the centuries. It dares to tackle the toughest questions about life: *Where do I go after I die? Is there a God? What do I do with my fears?* The Bible is the treasure map that leads to God's highest treasure—eternal life.

But how do you study the Bible? Countless copies of Scripture sit unread on bookshelves and nightstands simply because people don't know how to read it. What can you do to make the Bible real in your life?

The clearest answer is found in the words of Jesus: *"Ask and it will be given to you; seek and you will find; knock and the door will be opened to you"* (Matthew 7:7).

The first step in understanding the Bible is asking God to help you. You should read it prayerfully. If anyone understands God's Word, it is because of God and not the reader.

*"The Advocate, the Holy Spirit, whom the Father will send in my name, will teach you all things and will remind you of everything I have said to you"* (John 14:26).

Before reading the Bible, pray and invite God to speak to you. Don't go to Scripture looking for your idea, but go searching for his.

Not only should you read the Bible prayerfully, but you should also read it carefully. *"Seek and you will find"* is the pledge. The Bible is not a newspaper to be skimmed but rather a mine to be quarried. *"If you look for it as for silver and search for it as for hidden treasure, then you will understand the fear of the* LORD *and find the knowledge of God"* (Proverbs 2:4–5).

Any worthy find requires effort. The Bible is no exception. To understand the Bible, you don't have to be brilliant, but you must be willing to roll up your sleeves and search.

*"Do your best to present yourself to God as one approved, a worker who does not need to be ashamed and who correctly handles the word of truth"* (2 Timothy 2:15).

Here's a practical point. Study the Bible a bit at a time. Hunger is not satisfied by eating twenty-one meals in one sitting once a week. The body needs a steady diet to remain strong. So does the soul. When God sent food to his people in the wilderness, he didn't provide loaves already made. Instead, he sent them manna in the shape of *"thin flakes like frost on the ground"* (Exodus 16:14).

God gave manna in limited portions.

God sends spiritual food the same way. He opens the heavens with just enough nutrients for today's hunger. He provides *"a rule for this, a rule for that; a little here, a little there"* (Isaiah 28:10).

Don't be discouraged if your reading reaps a small harvest. Some days a lesser portion is all that is needed. What is important is to search every day for that day's message. A steady diet of God's Word over a lifetime builds a healthy soul and mind.

It's much like the little girl who returned from her first day at school feeling a bit dejected. Her mom asked, "Did you learn anything?"

"Apparently not enough," the girl responded. "I have to go back tomorrow, and the next day, and the next . . . "

Such is the case with learning. And such is the case with Bible study. Understanding comes little by little over a lifetime.

There is a third step in understanding the Bible. After the asking and seeking comes the knocking. After you ask and search, *"knock and the door will be opened to you"* (Matthew 7:7).

To knock is to stand at God's door. To make yourself available. To climb the steps, cross the porch, stand at the doorway, and volunteer. Knocking goes beyond the realm of thinking and into the realm of acting.

To knock is to ask, *What can I do? How can I obey? Where can I go?*

It's one thing to know what to do. It's another to do it. But for those who do it—those who choose to obey—a special reward awaits them.

*"Whoever looks intently into the perfect law that gives freedom, and continues in it—not forgetting what they have heard, but doing it—they will be blessed in what they do"* (James 1:25).

What a promise. Blessings come to those who do what they read in God's Word! It's the same with medicine. If you only read the label but ignore the pills, it won't help. It's the same with food. If you only read the recipe but never cook, you won't be fed. And it's the same with the Bible. If you only read the words but never obey, you'll never know the joy God has promised.

Ask. Search. Knock. Simple, isn't it? So why don't you give it a try? If you do, you'll see why the Bible is the most remarkable book in history.

# INTRODUCTION TO
## *The Book of Ephesians*

I've just witnessed a beautiful wedding. The most beautiful I've ever seen. That says a lot, since I've seen a lot. Ministers see many weddings. It's a perk of the profession.

Is there anything more elegant than a wedding? Candles bathe a chapel in gold. Loving families fill the pews. Groomsmen and bridesmaids descend the aisles with bouquets of newness and rings of promise. What an occasion.

And nothing quite compares with that moment when the bride stands at the top of the aisle. Arm entwined with her father's, she takes those final steps with him and steps toward a new life with her groom.

Ahh, the glory of a wedding. So to say I just saw the most beautiful one is no small thing. What made these nuptials so unforgettable? The groom. Usually the groom is not the star of the wedding. The fellow is typically upstaged by the girl. But this wedding was made special by the groom. It was enhanced by something he did.

And who he was made what he did even more startling. You see, he's a cowboy: a stocky fellow who went to college on a rodeo scholarship. But the one standing by me was not a macho calf roper, but a pinch-me-I'm-dreaming boy who'd never seen a bride so gorgeous.

He was composed as he walked down the aisle. He was fine as he took his place at the altar.

But when he saw the bride, he wept.

It was the moment he'd dreamed of. It was as if he'd been given life's greatest gift—a bride in all her beauty. By the way, those are the very words Paul uses to describe the church: a bride in all her beauty.

*"[Jesus] died so that he could give the church to himself like a bride in all her beauty. He died so that the church could be pure and without fault, with no evil or sin or any other wrong thing in it"* (Ephesians 5:27 NCV).

Ponder that verse. Jesus died for a bride. He died so he could be married. This passage anticipates the day when the groom will see his bride—when Christ will receive his church. Jesus' fondest longing will be fulfilled. His Bride will arrive.

The letter to the Ephesians celebrates the beauty of the church—the Bride of Christ. From our perspective the church isn't so pretty. We see the backbiting, the squabbling, the divisions. Heaven sees that, as well. But heaven sees more. Heaven sees the church as cleansed and made holy by Christ.

Heaven sees the church ascending to heaven. Heaven sees the Bride wearing the spotless gown of Jesus Christ.

It's enough to make one weep.

## AUTHOR AND DATE

Paul, who persecuted the early church before his life was radically altered by meeting the risen Jesus on the road to Damascus (see Acts 9:1–31). Paul founded the church in Ephesus during his second missionary journey c. AD 52 (see 18:19) and spent three years teaching there during his third missionary journey c. AD 54–56 (see 19:8–10). He ultimately left the city following an uprising by the local silversmiths, who were angry his teaching had led to a loss in their profits (see 19:23–31). Paul likely wrote the letter c. AD 60 from Rome, where he was imprisoned at the time, and intended it to be circulated to a number of churches in the region around Ephesus rather than to a specific community in the city. It was delivered by Tychicus, likely at the same time as Colossians and Philemon (see Ephesians 6:21–22).

## SITUATION

The general nature of Ephesians makes it difficult to determine the exact purpose for which Paul wrote the letter or the specific problems that he was seeking to resolve. However, if the letter was written at the same time as Colossians, it can be surmised that Paul was seeking to address the same types of problems in the Ephesian church as in the church in Colossae: the infiltration of false teachings. As with the letter of Colossians, Paul wished to stamp out this false teaching before it could do major damage, and, in the process, encourage the believers to recognize their high calling as children and heirs of God.

## KEY THEMES

- We have many spiritual blessings through Christ.
- Each believer is gifted through the Spirit of God.
- Our faith should work its way into all of our relationships.
- Our spiritual strength comes from God through his Word and our faith.

## KEY VERSE

*For it is by grace you have been saved, through faith—and this is not from yourselves, it is the gift of God (Ephesians 2:8).*

## CONTENTS

I. Spiritual Blessings (1:1–3:21)

II. Unity and the Christian Lifestyle (4:1–6:24)

# WHERE DO YOU BELONG?

*In Him also we have obtained an inheritance, being
predestined according to the purpose of Him who works
all things according to the counsel of His will.*
EPHESIANS 1:11 NKJV

# REFLECTION

Paul opens his letter with a glorious anthem of praise for all the blessings that believers have "in Christ." One blessing is that they belong to God's family—a community of faith. Think of a time when you felt a true sense of belonging to a community or group of people. Consider the atmosphere, circumstances, and purpose of the group. What did it feel like to belong?

# SITUATION

The apostle Paul had much invested in the church of Ephesus. For three years he had lived in the city, built relationships with members of the community, and provided a strong foundation for the church. Now, even though he was in prison, he wanted to encourage believers in the church (and in the surrounding region) to recognize the blessings God had given them by adopting them into his family. Paul also wanted to compel them to stay true to the message of the gospel he had taught them in the face of false teachings in their midst. He begins with an expression of praise to God—a reminder of how God has set the believers apart for his service.

# OBSERVATION

*Read Ephesians 1:1–14 from the New International Version or the New King James Version.*

NEW INTERNATIONAL VERSION

[1] Paul, an apostle of Christ Jesus by the will of God,

To God's holy people in Ephesus, the faithful in Christ Jesus:

[2] Grace and peace to you from God our Father and the Lord Jesus Christ.

[3] Praise be to the God and Father of our Lord Jesus Christ, who has blessed us in the heavenly realms with every spiritual blessing in Christ. [4] For he chose us in him before the creation of the world to be holy and blameless in his sight. In love [5] he predestined us for adoption to sonship through Jesus Christ, in accordance with his pleasure and will— [6] to the praise of his glorious grace, which he has freely given us in the One he loves. [7] In him we have redemption through his blood, the forgiveness of sins, in accordance with the riches of God's grace [8] that he lavished on us. With all wisdom and understanding, [9] he made known to us the mystery of his will according to his good pleasure, which he purposed in Christ, [10] to be put into effect when the times reach their fulfillment—to bring unity to all things in heaven and on earth under Christ.

[11] In him we were also chosen, having been predestined according to the plan of him who works out everything in conformity with the purpose of his will, [12] in order that we, who were the first to put our hope in Christ, might be for the praise of his glory. [13] And you also were included in Christ when you heard the message of truth, the gospel of your salvation. When you believed, you were marked in him with a seal, the promised Holy Spirit, [14] who is a deposit guaranteeing our inheritance until the redemption of those who are God's possession—to the praise of his glory.

NEW KING JAMES VERSION

[1] Paul, an apostle of Jesus Christ by the will of God,

To the saints who are in Ephesus, and faithful in Christ Jesus:

² Grace to you and peace from God our Father and the Lord Jesus Christ.

³ Blessed be the God and Father of our Lord Jesus Christ, who has blessed us with every spiritual blessing in the heavenly places in Christ, ⁴ just as He chose us in Him before the foundation of the world, that we should be holy and without blame before Him in love, ⁵ having predestined us to adoption as sons by Jesus Christ to Himself, according to the good pleasure of His will, ⁶ to the praise of the glory of His grace, by which He made us accepted in the Beloved.

⁷ In Him we have redemption through His blood, the forgiveness of sins, according to the riches of His grace ⁸ which He made to abound toward us in all wisdom and prudence, ⁹ having made known to us the mystery of His will, according to His good pleasure which He purposed in Himself, ¹⁰ that in the dispensation of the fullness of the times He might gather together in one all things in Christ, both which are in heaven and which are on earth—in Him. ¹¹ In Him also we have obtained an inheritance, being predestined according to the purpose of Him who works all things according to the counsel of His will, ¹² that we who first trusted in Christ should be to the praise of His glory.

¹³ In Him you also trusted, after you heard the word of truth, the gospel of your salvation; in whom also, having believed, you were sealed with the Holy Spirit of promise, ¹⁴ who is the guarantee of our inheritance until the redemption of the purchased possession, to the praise of His glory.

# EXPLORATION

**1.** What are some of the spiritual blessings you have in Christ?

_____

_____

_____

_____

**2.** God offers the forgiveness of sins through the blood of Christ. What difference should that make in your daily life?

_____

_____

_____

_____

_____

**3.** What is special about the fact that God deliberately chose to adopt you into his family?

_____

_____

_____

_____

_____

_____

**4.** For what reason did God choose to make you a member of his family?

_____

_____

_____

_____

_____

**5.** What does Paul say that God makes known to his people? What does this mean to you?

_____

_____

_____

_____

_____

**6.** In what way is the Holy Spirit God's mark of ownership on you?

_____

_____

_____

_____

# INSPIRATION

And you thought God adopted you because you were good looking. You thought he needed your money or your wisdom. Sorry. God adopted you simply because he wanted to. You were in his good will and pleasure. Knowing full well the trouble you would be and the price he would pay, he signed his name next to yours and changed your name to his and took you home. Your *Abba* adopted you and became your Father.

May I pause here for just a minute? Most of you are with me . . . but a couple of you are shaking your heads. I see those squinty eyes. You don't believe me, do you? You're waiting for the fine print. There's got to be a gimmick. You know life has no free lunch, so you're waiting for the check.

Your discomfort is obvious. Even here in God's living room, you never unwind. Others put on slippers, you put on a front. Others relax, you stiffen. Always on your best behavior, ever anxious that you'll slip up and God will notice and out you'll go.

I understand your anxiety. Our experience with people has taught us that what is promised and what is presented aren't always the same. And for some, the thought of trusting a heavenly Father is doubly difficult because your earthly father disappointed or mistreated you.

If such is the case, I urge you: Don't confuse your heavenly Father with the fathers you've seen on earth. Your Father in heaven isn't prone to headaches and temper tantrums. He doesn't hold you one day and hit you the next. The man who fathered you may play such games, but the God who loves you never will. (From *The Great House of God* by Max Lucado.)

# REACTION

**7.** What are some situations in your life where you have vividly felt you didn't belong?

_____

_____

_____

_____

**8.** How did you discover you were highly regarded by someone? What did that feel like? In what ways did it affect your actions?

_____

_____

_____

_____

**9.** What is the problem with comparing God as your heavenly Father with an earthly father?

_____

_____

_____

_____

**10.** What conclusions can you draw from the statement that God chose you "before the creation of the world" (Ephesians 1:4)?

_____

_____

_____

_____

**11.** In what ways do you bring praise to God's glory?

_____

_____

_____

**12.** Who in your life has exemplified God's grace to you? How did the person do this for you?

_____

_____

_____

# LIFE LESSONS

We experience "belonging" in many ways in modern life: playing on a sports team, participating in community at work, or joining any number of different types of clubs. The attraction of these connections illustrates just how badly we all long to belong. Yet what these earth-based groups offer in part, our heavenly Father offers in whole. We long to belong because we were designed to belong. However, until we know to _whom_ we belong, life will always lack a sense of ultimate purpose and direction. In Christ, we can experience true belonging. Acknowledging that God has chosen us and "owns" us begins a great adventure of freedom and service for Christ.

# DEVOTION

_Thank you, God, for choosing us. May we be spurred on by your love to do great works, and yet never substitute those works for your great grace. May we always hear your voice. Keep us amazed and mesmerized by what you have done for us._

# JOURNALING

How does it affect you personally to know that you are *valued* and *chosen* by God?

# FOR FURTHER READING

To complete the book of Ephesians during this twelve-part study, read Ephesians 1:1–14. For more Bible passages on being a member of God's family, read John 1:11–13; Romans 8:15–17; Galatians 3:26–4:7; and Hebrews 12:8–11.

# THE POWER OF YOUR FAITH

*I pray that the eyes of your heart may be enlightened in order
that you may know the hope to which he has called you . . .
and his incomparably great power for us who believe.*

EPHESIANS 1:18–19

# REFLECTION

*Power* and *faith* rarely appear together in the same sentence. We tend to think of faith as a trait that creates endurance, comfort, and perhaps influence with God. But powerful faith? Yet those who spend time with authentic faithful people discover there is power in faith—or, more accurately, power released by faith. Who are two or three people you know who exhibit a powerful faith in God? What is the evidence of their faith?

# SITUATION

Paul has just reminded his readers of all the blessings they have received by being members of God's family. In this next section of his letter, he goes on to pray for their ability to fully appreciate these truths and recognize the power their faith in Christ has provided to them. In most of Paul's letters, we find his common practice was to pray before, during, and after he wrote to a particular congregation. He often described the way he prayed for his readers—not casual or canned prayers, but deep longings expressed to God on their behalf. In this way, Paul provides us with wonderful examples of how we can also encourage one another in prayer.

# OBSERVATION

*Read Ephesians 1:15–23 from the New International
Version or the New King James Version.*

### New International Version

[15] For this reason, ever since I heard about your faith in the Lord Jesus
and your love for all God's people, [16] I have not stopped giving thanks for
you, remembering you in my prayers. [17] I keep asking that the God of our
Lord Jesus Christ, the glorious Father, may give you the Spirit of wisdom
and revelation, so that you may know him better. [18] I pray that the eyes
of your heart may be enlightened in order that you may know the hope
to which he has called you, the riches of his glorious inheritance in his
holy people, [19] and his incomparably great power for us who believe. That
power is the same as the mighty strength [20] he exerted when he raised
Christ from the dead and seated him at his right hand in the heavenly
realms, [21] far above all rule and authority, power and dominion, and
every name that is invoked, not only in the present age but also in the
one to come. [22] And God placed all things under his feet and appointed
him to be head over everything for the church, [23] which is his body, the
fullness of him who fills everything in every way.

### New King James Version

[15] Therefore I also, after I heard of your faith in the Lord Jesus and your
love for all the saints, [16] do not cease to give thanks for you, making mention of you in my prayers: [17] that the God of our Lord Jesus Christ, the
Father of glory, may give to you the spirit of wisdom and revelation in the
knowledge of Him, [18] the eyes of your understanding being enlightened;
that you may know what is the hope of His calling, what are the riches
of the glory of His inheritance in the saints, [19] and what is the exceeding
greatness of His power toward us who believe, according to the working
of His mighty power [20] which He worked in Christ when He raised Him
from the dead and seated Him at His right hand in the heavenly places,

²¹ far above all principality and power and might and dominion, and every name that is named, not only in this age but also in that which is to come.

²² And He put all things under His feet, and gave Him to be head over all things to the church, ²³ which is His body, the fullness of Him who fills all in all.

# EXPLORATION

**1.** What do you learn in these verses about the way Paul prayed?

_____

_____

_____

_____

_____

**2.** Why should having faith in Christ make a difference in your life?

_____

_____

_____

_____

**3.** Paul prayed for the believers to have a spirit of wisdom and revelation to know God better. How would you describe the process of knowing God better?

_____

_____

_____

_____

**4.** What promises of rich and glorious blessings from God do you hold on to in your life?

_____

_____

_____

_____

**5.** The same power that raised Christ from the dead works through your faith. In what way should you be using the power of your faith?

_____

_____

_____

_____

**6.** If God is over all authorities and powers in this world, why do you think evil rulers still exist?

_____

_____

_____

# INSPIRATION

When you believe in Christ, he works a miracle in you. "When you believed, you were marked in him with a seal, the promised Holy Spirit" (Ephesians 1:13). You are permanently purified and empowered by God himself. The message of Jesus to the religious person is simple: _It's not what you do. It's what I do. I have moved in._ In time, you can say with Paul, "I no longer live, but Christ lives in me" (Galatians 2:20). You are no longer a clunker, not even a clean clunker. You are a sleek Indianapolis Motor Speedway racing machine.

_But if that's true,_ you may be asking, _why do I still sputter? If I'm born again, why do I fall so often?_ Well, why did you fall so often after your first birth? Did you exit the womb wearing cross-trainers? Did you do the two-step on the day of your delivery? Of course not! When you started to walk, you fell more than you stood. Should you then expect anything different form your spiritual walk?

*But I fall so often,* you reply. *I question my salvation.* Again, return to your first birth. Didn't you stumble as you were learning to walk? And when you stumbled, did you question the validity of your physical birth? Did you, as a one-year-old fresh flopped on the floor, shake your head and think, *I have fallen again. I must not be human!*

Of course not. The stumbles of a toddler do not invalidate the act of birth. And the stumbles of a Christian do not annul his spiritual birth.

Do you understand what God has done? He has deposited a Christ seed in you. As it grows, you will change. It's not that sin has no more presence in your life, but rather that sin has no more power over your life. Temptation will pester you, but temptation will not master you. What hope this brings! . . .

Think of it this way. Suppose you, for most of your life, have had a heart condition. Your frail pumper restricts your activities. Each morning at work when the healthy employees take the stairs, you wait for the elevator.

But then comes the transplant. A healthy heart is placed within you. After recovery, you return to work and encounter the flight of stairs—the same flight of stairs you earlier avoided. By habit, you start for the elevator. But then you remember. You aren't the same person. You have a new heart. Within you dwells a new power.

Do you live like the old person or the new? Do you count yourself as having a new heart or old? You have a choice to make.

You might say, "I can't climb stairs; I'm too weak." Does your choice negate the presence of a new heart? Dismiss the work of the surgeon? No. Choosing the elevator would suggest only one fact—you haven't learned to trust your new power.

It takes time. But at some point, you've got to try those stairs. You've got to test the new ticker. You've got to experiment with the new you. For if you don't, you will run out of steam. (From *Next Door Savior* by Max Lucado.)

# REACTION

**7.** How does the analogy of a toddler falling often when learning to walk help you to understand a person's new spiritual life in Christ?

_____

_____

_____

_____

**8.** How does it help you to know that stumbles do not invalidate your spiritual birth?

_____

_____

_____

_____

**9.** What does it mean that God has deposited a "Christ seed" in you?

_____

_____

_____

_____

_____

**10.** How would you answer the question as to whether you live like the "old person or the new"? How does this come down to a choice you must make?

_____

_____

_____

_____

_____

**11.** As a believer, you have been given power in Christ. What are some ways you are demonstrating you trust in that power—that you are "trying those stairs"?

_____

_____

_____

**12.** How does it help you to know the same power within you is the power that raised Jesus from the dead and seated him on the heavenly throne (see Ephesians 1:19–20)?

_____

_____

_____

# LIFE LESSONS

Paul's prayer for the Ephesians offers a powerful outline for praying for other believers. We can ask God to grant them spiritual growth, not because they try harder but because God pours himself into them. We can pray that others will know God better. The "knowing" Paul speaks of here is not figuring God out or understanding him completely, but a settling into intimacy with him. We can pray the Holy Spirit will seal other believers, marking them as God's own people, and lead them to a fuller appreciation of the salvation they have in Jesus Christ.

# DEVOTION

_Blessed Lord and God, we come to you, aware that you rule our world. You became flesh, dwelled among us, saw us in our fallen state, and reached in and pulled us out. You offered us salvation and mercy, and we are ever thankful. Help us to understand today the power you have given to us through our faith and to use that power in this world for your glory._

# JOURNALING

In what ways are you using the power that God has given you to advance his purposes?

# FOR FURTHER READING

To complete the book of Ephesians during this twelve-part study, read Ephesians 1:15–23. For more Bible passages on the power God provides to believers in Christ, read Matthew 16:17–19; Mark 16:15–18; Luke 10:19–20; John 14:11–14; Acts 1:7–8; and 2 Corinthians 10:3–5.

# LESSON THREE

# HAVE MERCY!

*Because of his great love for us, God, who
is rich in mercy, made us alive with Christ
even when we were dead in transgressions—
it is by grace you have been saved.*
EPHESIANS 2:4–5

# REFLECTION

Imagine you are teaching a lesson on mercy to a children's class. What illustration from your life would you use to describe what it feels like to receive mercy? How would you explain what it is like to be merciful to someone? What does mercy mean to you?

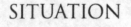

# SITUATION

Paul has laid the foundation for the new life and resurrection power that we receive when we come to faith in Christ. In this next section, he turns to discussing the actual transformation that takes place when we make this decision—how God brings us back to life from a place in which we were spiritually dead, raises us up, gives us power, and enables us to do good works for him. In this way, Paul distills the relationship between our faith in Christ, God's grace to us, and the actions that should then flow out of our salvation.

# OBSERVATION

*Read Ephesians 2:1–10 from the New International
Version or the New King James Version.*

## NEW INTERNATIONAL VERSION

[1] As for you, you were dead in your transgressions and sins, [2] in which you used to live when you followed the ways of this world and of the ruler of the kingdom of the air, the spirit who is now at work in those who are disobedient. [3] All of us also lived among them at one time, gratifying the cravings of our flesh and following its desires and thoughts. Like the rest, we were by nature deserving of wrath. [4] But because of his great love for us, God, who is rich in mercy, [5] made us alive with Christ even when we were dead in transgressions—it is by grace you have been saved. [6] And God raised us up with Christ and seated us with him in the heavenly realms in Christ Jesus, [7] in order that in the coming ages he might show the incomparable riches of his grace, expressed in his kindness to us in Christ Jesus. [8] For it is by grace you have been saved, through faith—and this is not from yourselves, it is the gift of God— [9] not by works, so that no one can boast. [10] For we are God's handiwork, created in Christ Jesus to do good works, which God prepared in advance for us to do.

## NEW KING JAMES VERSION

[1] And you He made alive, who were dead in trespasses and sins, [2] in which you once walked according to the course of this world, according to the prince of the power of the air, the spirit who now works in the sons of disobedience, [3] among whom also we all once conducted ourselves in the lusts of our flesh, fulfilling the desires of the flesh and of the mind, and were by nature children of wrath, just as the others.

[4] But God, who is rich in mercy, because of His great love with which He loved us, [5] even when we were dead in trespasses, made us alive together with Christ (by grace you have been saved), [6] and raised us up together, and made us sit together in the heavenly places in Christ Jesus,

[7] that in the ages to come He might show the exceeding riches of His grace in His kindness toward us in Christ Jesus. [8] For by grace you have been saved through faith, and that not of yourselves; it is the gift of God, [9] not of works, lest anyone should boast. [10] For we are His workmanship, created in Christ Jesus for good works, which God prepared beforehand that we should walk in them.

# EXPLORATION

**1.** In what sense is "spiritually dead" an accurate description of life without faith in Christ?

_____

_____

_____

**2.** How does accepting Christ signal a change in who has authority over you?

_____

_____

_____

**3.** What changes should occur in a person's life as a result of this new allegiance?

_____

_____

_____

**4.** What does it mean that you were "deserving of [God's] wrath" (verse 3)?

_____

_____

_____

**5.** What specific changes have occurred because of Christ's presence in your life?

_____

_____

_____

**6.** Why do you think believers sometimes perceive their salvation to be related to our own efforts? What does Paul say about this in verse 10?

_____

_____

_____

# INSPIRATION

Jesus was God's model of a human being. Ever honest in the midst of hypocrisy. Relentlessly kind in a world of cruelty. Heaven-focused in spite of countless distractions. When it came to sin, Jesus never did. We, on the other hand, have never stopped. We are "dead in trespasses and sins" and "strangers from the covenants of promise, having no hope and without God in the world" (Ephesians 2:1, 12 NKJV). We have nothing good to offer. Our finest deeds are rubbish and rags before a holy God (see Philippians 3:8; Isaiah 64:6). . . .

One of the most stinging indictments of humanity is found in Isaiah 53:6: "We all, like sheep, have gone astray, each of us has turned to his own way." . . . This is an unpopular yet essential truth. All ships that land at the shore of grace weigh anchor from the port of sin. We must start where God starts. We won't appreciate what grace does until we understand who we are. We are rebels. We are Barabbas. Like him, we deserve to die. Four prison walls, thickened with fear, hurt, and hate, surround us.

We are incarcerated by our past, our low-road choices, and our high-minded pride. We have been found guilty. We sit on the floor of the

25

dusty cell, awaiting the final moment. Our executioner's footsteps echo against stone walls. Head between knees, we don't look up as he opens the door; we don't lift our eyes as he begins to speak. We know what he is going to say. "Time to pay for your sins." But we hear something else.

"You're free to go. They took Jesus instead of you."

The door swings open, the guard barks, "Get out," and we find ourselves in the light of the morning sun, shackles gone, crimes pardoned, wondering, *What just happened?*

Grace happened.

Christ took away your sins. Where did he take them? To the top of a hill called Calvary, where he endured not just the nails of the Romans, the mockery of the crowd, and the spear of the soldier but the anger of God. (From *Grace* by Max Lucado.)

# REACTION

**7.** How does the image of a prison cell describe your life before coming to Christ?

_____

_____

_____

_____

**8.** What would your life be like if God hadn't extended mercy to you?

_____

_____

_____

**9.** When was a time you had the opportunity to show mercy but didn't? Why didn't you?

_____

_____

_____

**10.** What is an act mercy you have seen recently from another person?

_____

_____

_____

_____

**11.** What is the danger of a faith based solely on works? How do you tell the difference between works-based faith and faith-based works?

_____

_____

_____

_____

**12.** How can you, as a Christian, show the great riches of God's grace?

_____

_____

_____

_____

# LIFE LESSONS

In an imperfect world, we tend to think our rewards are connected to our performance. Those who don't try or don't work hard shouldn't get the same benefits as those who do try and work hard. But when we apply this thinking to a perfect God with absolute standards, our meager efforts don't make the grade. Without God's mercy and grace, we're stuck in imperfect. We're stuck without hope. We're just plain *stuck*. But God's mercy comes and gets us unstuck. His mercy saves us through Jesus Christ. And since we continue to live in an imperfect world where we continue to experience falling short, God's mercy *continues* to get us unstuck.

# DEVOTION

*Father, we call ourselves your people, and yet we carry the baggage of a week of concerns. We come to you just as we are, without trying to hide our mistakes and our weaknesses. We need your mercy and grace. Lord, mend us and make us better than we could be alone.*

# JOURNALING

What are some ways I can show more mercy to others through my life?

_____

_____

_____

_____

_____

_____

_____

_____

_____

_____

_____

# FOR FURTHER READING

To complete the book of Ephesians during this twelve-part study, read Ephesians 2:1–10. For more Bible passages on God's mercy, read Nehemiah 9:29–31; Joel 2:12–14; Micah 7:18–20; Luke 6:34–36; 1 Timothy 1:15–16; and Titus 3:3–8.

# FAMILY TIES AND RACIAL BLURS

*You are no longer strangers and foreigners,*
*but fellow citizens with the saints and*
*members of the household of God.*

EPHESIANS 2:19 NKJV

# REFLECTION

In Paul's day the early Christians wrestled with prejudice and racism and pride. In our day people in the church are not perfect either. For a few moments, consider the relationships you have within the family of God. Do you put up walls and barriers? How have the good parts of these relationships and experiences shaped you as a person?

# SITUATION

In most cities where Christianity was planted, society was divided into two groups: displaced Jews and everyone else (Gentiles). The region surrounding Ephesus was no exception. Often, an uneasy truce held in these cities between the groups for the sake of business or peace. However, as Paul will now address, the gospel created new unexpected tensions. This was because Christianity removed the natural social and religious barriers between the groups. While this was not always a welcomed development, Paul consistently teaching that, in Christ, people from very different backgrounds can all be one in God's family.

# OBSERVATION

*Read Ephesians 2:11–22 from the New International*
*Version or the New King James Version.*

## NEW INTERNATIONAL VERSION

[11] Therefore, remember that formerly you who are Gentiles by birth and called "uncircumcised" by those who call themselves "the circumcision" (which is done in the body by human hands)— [12] remember that at that time you were separate from Christ, excluded from citizenship in Israel and foreigners to the covenants of the promise, without hope and without God in the world. [13] But now in Christ Jesus you who once were far away have been brought near by the blood of Christ.

[14] For he himself is our peace, who has made the two groups one and has destroyed the barrier, the dividing wall of hostility, [15] by setting aside in his flesh the law with its commands and regulations. His purpose was to create in himself one new humanity out of the two, thus making peace, [16] and in one body to reconcile both of them to God through the cross, by which he put to death their hostility. [17] He came and preached peace to you who were far away and peace to those who were near. [18] For through him we both have access to the Father by one Spirit.

[19] Consequently, you are no longer foreigners and strangers, but fellow citizens with God's people and also members of his household, [20] built on the foundation of the apostles and prophets, with Christ Jesus himself as the chief cornerstone. [21] In him the whole building is joined together and rises to become a holy temple in the Lord. [22] And in him you too are being built together to become a dwelling in which God lives by his Spirit.

## NEW KING JAMES VERSION

[11] Therefore remember that you, once Gentiles in the flesh—who are called Uncircumcision by what is called the Circumcision made in the flesh by hands— [12] that at that time you were without Christ, being aliens from the commonwealth of Israel and strangers from the covenants of

31

promise, having no hope and without God in the world. <sup>13</sup> But now in Christ Jesus you who once were far off have been brought near by the blood of Christ.

<sup>14</sup> For He Himself is our peace, who has made both one, and has broken down the middle wall of separation, <sup>15</sup> having abolished in His flesh the enmity, that is, the law of commandments contained in ordinances, so as to create in Himself one new man from the two, thus making peace, <sup>16</sup> and that He might reconcile them both to God in one body through the cross, thereby putting to death the enmity. <sup>17</sup> And He came and preached peace to you who were afar off and to those who were near. <sup>18</sup> For through Him we both have access by one Spirit to the Father.

<sup>19</sup> Now, therefore, you are no longer strangers and foreigners, but fellow citizens with the saints and members of the household of God, <sup>20</sup> having been built on the foundation of the apostles and prophets, Jesus Christ Himself being the chief cornerstone, <sup>21</sup> in whom the whole building, being fitted together, grows into a holy temple in the Lord, <sup>22</sup> in whom you also are being built together for a dwelling place of God in the Spirit.

# EXPLORATION

**1.** What are some of the divisions that would have existed between Jews and Gentiles?

_____

_____

_____

**2.** What does Paul mean when he says the Gentiles were "foreigners to the covenants of the promise" (verse 12)? How did this change when they accepted Christ?

_____

_____

_____

**3.** What is Paul describing when he says that Christ is your peace?

_____

_____

_____

**4.** Before Christ, the Jewish nation judged their righteousness by their obedience to numerous laws and regulations. How did Christ's life and death challenge that concept of righteousness?

_____

_____

_____

**5.** Christ's death and resurrection changed the way people approach God—from his creatures to his children. How would you describe the difference (see also Romans 8:13–17)?

_____

_____

_____

**6.** Paul describes the church by comparing it to a building constructed of many stones. How does that analogy work well in describing the church today?

_____

_____

_____

# INSPIRATION

We specialize in "I am right" rallies. We write books about what the other does wrong. We major in finding gossip and become experts in unveiling weaknesses. We split into little huddles and then, God forbid, we split again . . .

Are our differences that divisive? Are our opinions that obtrusive? Are our walls that wide? Is it *that* impossible to find a common cause?

"May they all be one," Jesus prayed.

One. Not one in groups of two thousand. But one in One. *One* church. *One* faith. *One* Lord. Not Baptist, not Methodist, not Adventist. Just Christian. No denominations. No hierarchies. No traditions. Just Christ.

Too idealistic? Impossible to achieve? I don't think so. Harder things have been done, you know. For example, once upon a tree, a Creator gave his life for his creation. Maybe all we need are a few hearts that are willing to follow suit. (From *No Wonder They Call Him the Savior* by Max Lucado.)

# REACTION

**7.** What are some of benefits you have discovered in belonging to God's family?

_____

_____

_____

_____

**8.** How did Christ's death give you the right to come to God as your father?

_____

_____

_____

_____

**9.** What were the racial implications of the peace that Christ brought?

_____

_____

_____

_____

**10.** One of Jesus' efforts was to end racially and culturally based hatred. In what ways can the church today help in that same effort?

_____

_____

_____

_____

**11.** What barriers to unity in Christ have you seen in your own church?

_____

_____

_____

**12.** What is important about the fact that Jesus is the cornerstone of the church? How can that lead to more unity among believers?

_____

_____

_____

## LIFE LESSONS

Jesus ended his Sermon on the Mount with the claim that trusting and obeying him was like building a house on a rock (see Matthew 7:24–27). Paul echoes that point in his teaching about the church. Everything rests on Jesus Christ. Faithfulness to him determines all actions and decisions. Jesus is the ultimate equalizer. In a world where we are proud of what makes us different/better than others, Jesus offers a place where we meet as equals. He declares the walls we build are irrelevant—and he wants to remove them. Jesus doesn't offer an alternative; he comes to us with the original plan and a way to get back to it. He is the way.

# DEVOTION

*Father, as we set about the task of being your people, we pray that you will help us. May we glorify your name. May we be open-minded. May we be sincere. May we be willing to change and grow. We thank you, Lord, for the privilege of being in your family.*

# JOURNALING

What are your privileges and responsibilities in belonging to God's family?

# FOR FURTHER READING

To complete the book of Ephesians during this twelve-part study, read Ephesians 2:11–22. For more Bible passages on God's family, read Acts 13:44–48; Romans 8:13–17; 2 Corinthians 5:14–15; Galatians 3:26–29; and 1 Timothy 2:3–4.

# LESSON FIVE

# GOD HAD A SECRET?

*This grace was given me: to preach to the Gentiles*
*the boundless riches of Christ, and to make plain*
*to everyone the administration of this mystery,*
*which for ages past was kept hidden in God.*
EPHESIANS 3:8–9

# REFLECTION

Secrets and mysteries are selective—they are only secrets and mysteries to the ones who don't know about them! God has always known his plans, and he has graciously shared them with his creation in his timing. Think of a time when someone gave you a surprise party or gift that he or she had worked on in secret. How did you feel when you received it?

_____

_____

_____

_____

# SITUATION

Throughout Paul's letters, he often spoke confidently about the oneness that all believers—whether formerly Jew or Gentile—share in Christ Jesus. As relates in this next part of his letter, one of the primary reasons for his assurance was his training in the Old Testament Scriptures. Paul realized the gospel message, with its inclusion of Gentiles, had always been there. It was there in plain sight, but it took Jesus to finally reveal it to the world. God's plan for all people, once mysterious and "hidden," has been made available for all people to know and understand.

# OBSERVATION

*Read Ephesians 3:1–13 from the New International*
*Version or the New King James Version.*

NEW INTERNATIONAL VERSION
¹ For this reason I, Paul, the prisoner of Christ Jesus for the sake of you Gentiles—

[2] Surely you have heard about the administration of God's grace that was given to me for you, [3] that is, the mystery made known to me by revelation, as I have already written briefly. [4] In reading this, then, you will be able to understand my insight into the mystery of Christ, [5] which was not made known to people in other generations as it has now been revealed by the Spirit to God's holy apostles and prophets. [6] This mystery is that through the gospel the Gentiles are heirs together with Israel, members together of one body, and sharers together in the promise in Christ Jesus.

[7] I became a servant of this gospel by the gift of God's grace given me through the working of his power. [8] Although I am less than the least of all the Lord's people, this grace was given me: to preach to the Gentiles the boundless riches of Christ, [9] and to make plain to everyone the administration of this mystery, which for ages past was kept hidden in God, who created all things. [10] His intent was that now, through the church, the manifold wisdom of God should be made known to the rulers and authorities in the heavenly realms, [11] according to his eternal purpose that he accomplished in Christ Jesus our Lord. [12] In him and through faith in him we may approach God with freedom and confidence. [13] I ask you, therefore, not to be discouraged because of my sufferings for you, which are your glory.

## NEW KING JAMES VERSION

[1] For this reason I, Paul, the prisoner of Christ Jesus for you Gentiles— [2] if indeed you have heard of the dispensation of the grace of God which was given to me for you, [3] how that by revelation He made known to me the mystery (as I have briefly written already, [4] by which, when you read, you may understand my knowledge in the mystery of Christ), [5] which in other ages was not made known to the sons of men, as it has now been revealed by the Spirit to His holy apostles and prophets: [6] that the Gentiles should be fellow heirs, of the same body, and partakers of His promise in Christ through the gospel, [7] of which I became a minister according to the gift of the grace of God given to me by the effective working of His power.

⁸ To me, who am less than the least of all the saints, this grace was given, that I should preach among the Gentiles the unsearchable riches of Christ, ⁹ and to make all see what is the fellowship of the mystery, which from the beginning of the ages has been hidden in God who created all things through Jesus Christ; ¹⁰ to the intent that now the manifold wisdom of God might be made known by the church to the principalities and powers in the heavenly places, ¹¹ according to the eternal purpose which He accomplished in Christ Jesus our Lord, ¹² in whom we have boldness and access with confidence through faith in Him. ¹³ Therefore I ask that you do not lose heart at my tribulations for you, which is your glory.

# EXPLORATION

**1.** Paul, a Jew, became a missionary to the Gentiles at a time when the Jewish people found their identity in the fact they were God's only chosen people. What consequences might Paul have had to pay for his actions (see 2 Corinthians 11:16–33)?

_____

_____

_____

_____

**2.** Why did Paul describe God's plan—to offer all people salvation—as a "secret"?

_____

_____

_____

**3.** Why might the Jewish leaders have felt threatened by Paul's insistence that God included all people in his promise of salvation?

_____

_____

_____

**4.** How does Paul describe the way in which he became "a servant of this gospel" to the Gentiles (verse 7)?

_God's grace (honored)_

**5.** Why do you think Paul states he is "less than the least of the Lord's people" (verse 8)?

**6.** What role does the church play in revealing God's plan of salvation to the world?

# INSPIRATION

_What would it be like to become flesh?_ This question surfaced once as I was golfing. Waiting my turn to putt, I squatted down to clean my ball and noticed a mountain of ants beside it. Must have been dozens of them, all over each other. A pyramid of motion at least half an inch tall.

I don't know what you think when you see ants on a green as you are waiting to putt. But here is what I thought: _Why are you guys all bunched up? You have the whole green. Why, the entire golf course in yours to spread out in._

Then it occurred to me. These ants are nervous. Who could blame them? They live under a constant meteor shower. Every few minutes a dimpled orb comes crashing into their world. Bam! Bam! Bam! Just when the bombing stops, the mallet-swinging giants arrive. If you survive their feet and sticks, they roll a meteor at you. A golf green is no place for an ant.

So I tried to help them. Leaning down where they could hear me, I invited, "Come on, follow me. We'll find a nice spot in the rough. I know it well." Not one looked in my direction. "Hey, ants!" Still no reply. Then I realized, I don't speak their language. I don't speak Ant. Pretty fluent in the idiom of Uncle, but I don't speak Ant.

So what could I do to reach them? Only one thing. I needed to become an ant. Go from six feet two inches to teeny-weeny. From 200-plus pounds to tenths of an ounce. Swap my big world for their tiny one. Give up burgers and start eating grass. "No thanks," I said. Besides, it was my turn to putt.

Love goes the distance . . . and Christ traveled from limitless eternity to be confined by time in order to become one of us. He didn't have to. He could have given up. At any step along the way he could have called it quits . . . but he didn't, because he is love.

"[Love] endures all things" (1 Corinthians 13:7 NKJV). Jesus endured the distance. (From *A Love Worth Giving* by Max Lucado.)

# REACTION

**7.** Why was it necessary in God's plan of salvation for Jesus to come into this world?

_____

_____

_____

_____

_____

**8.** The secret of God's salvation is really too great for human beings to fully understand. On what, then, do you base your faith in God's salvation?

_____

_____

_____

_____

**9.** What are some examples in your everyday world of things you use or benefit from, even though you do not understand them?

_____

_____

_____

**10.** How would you describe God's love to someone who has never heard of God?

_____

_____

_____

**11.** How does it make you feel to know that God had a plan for you to come to him?

_____

_____

_____

**12.** How have you experienced the riches of Christ in your life?

_____

_____

_____

## LIFE LESSONS

We function every day making use of items whose workings we don't understand. We drive cars, use copiers, type on computers, and perform many other tasks with only a dim sense of what makes a car run, a copier copy, or a computer compute. The same is true of the mystery of being in Christ. We don't have to fully understand God's grace before we take full advantage of it. We don't have to comprehend (and certainly never will on this side of eternity) why God loves us, but that should never keep us from experiencing and relishing in his love.

# DEVOTION

*Father, we look at your plan and see that it's all based on your love, not on our performance. Help us understand this. Teach us to be captivated by your love. Allow us to be overwhelmed by your grace. Remind us to live grateful lives. Amen.*

# JOURNALING

In what situations or times your life have you felt the most loved by God?

_____

_____

_____

_____

_____

_____

_____

_____

_____

_____

# FOR FURTHER READING

To complete the book of Ephesians during this twelve-part study, read Ephesians 3:1–13. For more Bible passages on God's provision through Christ, read John 3:16; 15:12; Romans 5:8; 8:35–37; and 1 John 3:1.

# THE AMAZING LOVE OF CHRIST

*May [you] have power, together with all the Lord's holy people,*
*to grasp how wide and long and high and deep is the love*
*of Christ, and to know this love that surpasses knowledge.*
EPHESIANS 3:18–19

# REFLECTION

You can't see love, or touch it, but it is nevertheless a powerful force. When was the last time you were truly amazed by someone's love for you? How would you describe that experience?

_____

_____

_____

_____

_____

# SITUATION

Among the personal traits that Paul reveals in his letters, one stands out clearly: he was always praying. Paul began this letter with prayer, and now, as he concludes the teaching part of his message, he prays for the Ephesians again. Where earlier he praised the believers for the love they showed to one another, here he describes the incredible love that Christ has for them—a love that is so wide, long, high, and deep, that it impossible for humans to grasp!

# OBSERVATION

*Read Ephesians 3:14–21 from the New International Version or the New King James Version.*

New International Version

¹⁴ For this reason I kneel before the Father, ¹⁵ from whom every family in heaven and on earth derives its name. ¹⁶ I pray that out of his glorious riches he may strengthen you with power through his Spirit in your

inner being, [17] so that Christ may dwell in your hearts through faith. And I pray that you, being rooted and established in love, [18] may have power, together with all the Lord's holy people, to grasp how wide and long and high and deep is the love of Christ, [19] and to know this love that surpasses knowledge—that you may be filled to the measure of all the fullness of God.

[20] Now to him who is able to do immeasurably more than all we ask or imagine, according to his power that is at work within us, [21] to him be glory in the church and in Christ Jesus throughout all generations, for ever and ever! Amen.

## NEW KING JAMES VERSION

[14] For this reason I bow my knees to the Father of our Lord Jesus Christ, [15] from whom the whole family in heaven and earth is named, [16] that He would grant you, according to the riches of His glory, to be strengthened with might through His Spirit in the inner man, [17] that Christ may dwell in your hearts through faith; that you, being rooted and grounded in love, [18] may be able to comprehend with all the saints what is the width and length and depth and height— [19] to know the love of Christ which passes knowledge; that you may be filled with all the fullness of God.

[20] Now to Him who is able to do exceedingly abundantly above all that we ask or think, according to the power that works in us, [21] to Him be glory in the church by Christ Jesus to all generations, forever and ever. Amen.

# EXPLORATION

**1.** In what way does every family on heaven and earth get their true "name" from God?

_____

_____

_____

**2.** Paul prayed the Ephesian believers would be "strong inwardly" through Christ's Spirit. Who is a person you know who fits that description?

_____

_____

_____

**3.** What does it mean to be rooted and established in God's love?

_____

_____

_____

**4.** What are the hallmarks of families and churches when they are built on God's love?

_____

_____

_____

**5.** In what ways can you know Christ's love—even though you can fully understand it?

_____

_____

_____

**6.** How can you be sure God's power, rather than your own strength, is working through you?

_____

_____

_____

_____

# INSPIRATION

Peek through the Nazareth workshop window. See the lanky lad sweeping the sawdust from the floor? He once blew stardust into the night sky. Why swap the heavens for a carpentry shop? One answer: *love*. Love explains why he came. Love explains how he endured. . . .

"Observe how Christ loved us. . . . He didn't love in order to get something from us but to give everything of himself to us" (Ephesians 5:2 MSG). Your goodness can't win God's love. Nor can your badness lose it. But you can resist it. We tend to do so honestly. . . .

Like my old dog Salty. He was a cranky cuss, but I liked him. He was a wiry canine by nature—shave his salt-and-pepper mop, and he'd pass for a bulimic Chihuahua. He didn't have much to start with, but over the years the seasons took his energy, teeth, hearing, and all but eighteen inches' worth of eyesight. Toss him a dog treat, and he would just stare at the floor through cloudy cataracts. (Or, in his case, dogaracts?) He was nervous and edgy, quick to growl and slow to trust. As I reached out to pet him, he yanked back. Still, I petted the old coot. I knew he couldn't see, and I could only wonder how dark his world had become.

We are a lot like Salty. I have a feeling that most people who defy and deny God do so more out of fear than conviction. For all our chest pumping and braggadocio, we are anxious folk—can't see a step into the future, can't hear the one who owns us. No wonder we try to gum the hand that feeds us. But God reaches and touches. . . .

Mark it down: He loves you with an unearthly love. You can't win it by being winsome. You can't lose it by being a loser. But you can be blind enough to resist it. Don't. For heaven's sake, don't. For your sake, don't. "Take in with all [Christians] the extravagant dimensions of Christ's love. Reach out and experience the breadth! Test its length! Plumb the depths! Rise to the heights! Live full lives, full in the fullness of God" (Ephesians 3:18–19 MSG).

Others demote you. God claims you. Let the definitive voice of the universe say, "You're still a part of my plan" (From *3:16: The Numbers of Hope* by Max Lucado.)

# REACTION

**7.** How do you respond to the idea you can't win Jesus' love, or lose it, but you can resist it?

**8.** Why do so many people today resist Christ's love? What do you think they fear?

**9.** What are some ways Jesus showed his love and compassion during his earthly ministry (for example, see Matthew 9:36–38; 20:29–34; and Luke 8:40–56)?

**10.** What ministries in the church today reflect the way Jesus cared for the people around him?

**11.** How do you respond when you consider the depth of love that Jesus has for you?

_____

_____

_____

_____

**12.** How can you build your life on that love and share it with others?

_____

_____

_____

_____

## LIFE LESSONS

We can't force people to believe God loves them, and they can't stop *us* from loving them. The underlying power of Paul's words to the Ephesian believers came from the convincing power of the Holy Spirit and from the compassionate power of his commitment to them. God's love has a width, length, height, and depth, but we will never reach the end of it. Our capacity to experience God's love will be exhausted long before God's capacity to give it is strained. The picture of having Christ "dwell" inside us by faith presents us with compelling and comforting possibilities. What Christ does in us and through us will always be "exceedingly abundantly above all that we ask or think" (Ephesians 3:20 NKJV).

## DEVOTION

*We're not perfect, Father, but we are yours. We claim your salvation and your grace. We ask you to make us every day into the image of Jesus Christ. Help us to walk this earth in love as he did. We are amazed at such mercy that forgives us time and time again. Thank you.*

# JOURNALING

How can you be more like Christ in the way you show love to the people around you?

_____

_____

_____

_____

_____

_____

_____

_____

_____

_____

_____

_____

_____

_____

_____

_____

_____

# FOR FURTHER READING

To complete the book of Ephesians during this twelve-part study, read Ephesians 3:14–21. For more Bible passages on Christ's love, read Matthew 8:14–16; 14:13–14; 23:37; Mark 10:13–16; Luke 7:12–13; 22:49–51; and John 11:33–35.

# BODY PARTS
# EVERYWHERE

*He Himself gave some to be apostles, some prophets,*
*some evangelists, and some pastors and teachers,*
*for the equipping of the saints for the work of*
*ministry, for the edifying of the body of Christ.*
EPHESIANS 4:11–12 NKJV

# REFLECTION

Injuries, broken bones, and the loss of limb can have a devastating effect on a person's body. Even a simple blister on a toe or paper cut on a finger can quickly reminds you how much you use every part of your anatomy to function. Consider for a few moments how valuable each part of your body is to you. Why is the body of Christ such a meaningful analogy for the church?

# SITUATION

In the next portion of Paul's letter, he moves from talking about the wonders of God and the Christian life to showing believers how to put these concepts into practice in their lives. It's as if he were saying to them, "If you agree with what I've just told you, then the following choices and actions on your part will be required." The first item Paul asks them to put into practice is loving one another in the church—and recognizing that each person has value and a purpose.

# OBSERVATION

*Read Ephesians 4:1–16 from the New International
Version or the New King James Version.*

NEW INTERNATIONAL VERSION

[1] As a prisoner for the Lord, then, I urge you to live a life worthy of the calling you have received. [2] Be completely humble and gentle; be patient, bearing with one another in love. [3] Make every effort to keep the unity of the Spirit through the bond of peace. [4] There is one body and one Spirit, just as you were called to one hope when you were called; [5] one Lord, one faith, one baptism; [6] one God and Father of all, who is over all and through all and in all.

[7] But to each one of us grace has been given as Christ apportioned it. [8] This is why it says:

> "When he ascended on high,
>     he took many captives
>     and gave gifts to his people."

[9] (What does "he ascended" mean except that he also descended to the lower, earthly regions? [10] He who descended is the very one who ascended higher than all the heavens, in order to fill the whole universe.) [11] So Christ himself gave the apostles, the prophets, the evangelists, the pastors and teachers, [12] to equip his people for works of service, so that the body of Christ may be built up [13] until we all reach unity in the faith and in the knowledge of the Son of God and become mature, attaining to the whole measure of the fullness of Christ.

[14] Then we will no longer be infants, tossed back and forth by the waves, and blown here and there by every wind of teaching and by the cunning and craftiness of people in their deceitful scheming. [15] Instead, speaking the truth in love, we will grow to become in every respect the mature body of him who is the head, that is, Christ. [16] From him the

whole body, joined and held together by every supporting ligament, grows and builds itself up in love, as each part does its work.

NEW KING JAMES VERSION

[1] I, therefore, the prisoner of the Lord, beseech you to walk worthy of the calling with which you were called, [2] with all lowliness and gentleness, with longsuffering, bearing with one another in love, [3] endeavoring to keep the unity of the Spirit in the bond of peace. [4] There is one body and one Spirit, just as you were called in one hope of your calling; [5] one Lord, one faith, one baptism; [6] one God and Father of all, who is above all, and through all, and in you all.

[7] But to each one of us grace was given according to the measure of Christ's gift. [8] Therefore He says:

> "When He ascended on high,
> He led captivity captive,
> And gave gifts to men."

[9] (Now this, "He ascended"—what does it mean but that He also first descended into the lower parts of the earth? [10] He who descended is also the One who ascended far above all the heavens, that He might fill all things.)

[11] And He Himself gave some to be apostles, some prophets, some evangelists, and some pastors and teachers, [12] for the equipping of the saints for the work of ministry, for the edifying of the body of Christ, [13] till we all come to the unity of the faith and of the knowledge of the Son of God, to a perfect man, to the measure of the stature of the fullness of Christ; [14] that we should no longer be children, tossed to and fro and carried about with every wind of doctrine, by the trickery of men, in the cunning craftiness of deceitful plotting, [15] but, speaking the truth in love, may grow up in all things into Him who is the head—Christ— [16] from whom the whole body, joined and knit together by what every joint supplies, according to the effective working by which every part does its share, causes growth of the body for the edifying of itself in love.

# EXPLORATION

**1.** What does Paul mean when he urges the believers in Ephesus to live "worthy of the calling" they have received (verse 1)? How would you describe the life that God calls you to live?

_____

_____

_____

_____

**2.** What are some ways Christians can accept one another and bear with one another in love?

_____

_____

_____

_____

**3.** How is this acceptance affected when believers encounter someone they don't like?

_____

_____

_____

_____

**4.** Paul notes that followers of Jesus have been given a special gift of grace. Have you identified your own gift of grace? If not, what steps can you take to do so?

_____

_____

_____

_____

**5.** The purpose of the gifts God has given to you is to help you grow to maturity in Christ. In what ways do the gifts you have identified help you do this?

_____

_____

_____

_____

**6.** Paul compares the church to a body. What part of the body are you?

_____

_____

_____

# INSPIRATION

What would happen if, as you went to work, your stomach decided to stay home and take a little break? Or your spleen decided it just needed some time to get its act together? Or if your left foot decided to just walk out on you?

You would be a mess. Practically dead. Completely incapacitated.

Ever wonder why Paul so often refers to the church as the body of Christ? "God has placed the parts in the body, every one of them, just as he wanted them to be" (1 Corinthians 12:18). "[Jesus] is the head of the body, the church" (Colossians 1:18). "From [Christ] the whole body, joined and held together by every supporting ligament, grows and builds itself up in love, as each part does its work" (Ephesians 4:16).

I am not his body. You are not his body. We—_together_—are his body. . . . Every part of the body is necessary because each serves a function. No part is the whole, but every part is part of the whole. Our world desperately needs people who stick together and love one another. This group is the church.

Is there ever a time to leave a church? Yes. In the event of immoral or dishonest leadership. If the pastors are using or abusing the flock, get out. Otherwise, brains need to find reasonable answers, eyes need to see the problems, stomachs need to digest the situation, spleens need to get rid of bacteria, hands need to soothe, and feet need to get to work.

Don't eject yourself from the body . . . or it will die. (Adapted from *Max on Life* by Max Lucado.)

# REACTION

**7.** Why is it so important for believers to use their gifts in the church?

_____

_____

_____

_____

**8.** What role do you see your particular gifts playing in your church?

_____

_____

_____

_____

**9.** In what ways are you using your gifts to build up the body of Christ?

_____

_____

_____

**10.** What are some ways you have chosen to stick together with your church body and work through particular issues that have arisen?

_____

_____

_____

**11.** What does it mean that Christ is the "head" on the church body?

_____

_____

_____

_____

**12.** What keeps believers from exhibiting humility, gentleness, and patience with one another and becoming one as Paul instructs in this passage?

_____

_____

_____

## LIFE LESSONS

The Christian life means following the One who calls us. That life has a basic outline, sketched by God. It can be described as a central collection of beliefs and gifts. The beliefs are shared in common; the gifts are given individually for the common good. The daily challenge for us as believers is to participate in life in a worthy way because of all that we have been given in Christ. All believers contribute to the body of Christ. Some of their specific roles, primarily those in leadership, require faithfulness, courage, and the cooperation of those being led. The life challenge for a Christian involves a mixture of personal spiritual responsibility and willing cooperation with other believers. We share our gifts and benefit from theirs.

## DEVOTION

_Father, you have been so good to us and have given us so many gifts to use in your body. Help us to share our gifts freely with others and always seek to be one in Christ. Help us to be busy about the right business—the business of serving you._

# JOURNALING

What are some ways that you could offer to use your gifts in your church this week?

# FOR FURTHER READING

To complete the book of Ephesians during this twelve-part study, read Ephesians 4:1–16. For more Bible passages on the purpose of our gifts, read Romans 12:3–6; 1 Corinthians 12:12; 14:26; 1 Timothy 4:14; and 2 Timothy 1:6.

# THE POWER OF WORDS

*Let no corrupt word proceed out of your mouth,*
*but what is good for necessary edification,*
*that it may impart grace to the hearers.*
EPHESIANS 4:29 NKJV

# REFLECTION

Think of a time when someone's careless words hurt you (or vice versa). What was the immediate effect on both of you? How was the offense resolved?

_____

_____

_____

_____

_____

# SITUATION

Paul understood that most of the believers in Ephesus had come from a culture that worshiped many different gods. The Temple of Artemis (or Diana) in Ephesus ranked as one of the seven wonders of the ancient world, and visitors flocked there to worship the goddess and buy silver trinkets (see Acts 19:24). Paul also knew that for the body of Christ to function and for its members to operate in their gifts, they had to "put off" the behaviors of their former lives that were incompatible with their new lives in Christ—including speaking falsehoods and promoting unwholesome talk. He seeks to address these particular issues next.

# OBSERVATION

_Read Ephesians 4:17–32 from the New International Version or the New King James Version._

NEW INTERNATIONAL VERSION

¹⁷ So I tell you this, and insist on it in the Lord, that you must no longer live as the Gentiles do, in the futility of their thinking. ¹⁸ They are darkened

in their understanding and separated from the life of God because of the ignorance that is in them due to the hardening of their hearts. [19] Having lost all sensitivity, they have given themselves over to sensuality so as to indulge in every kind of impurity, and they are full of greed.

[20] That, however, is not the way of life you learned [21] when you heard about Christ and were taught in him in accordance with the truth that is in Jesus. [22] You were taught, with regard to your former way of life, to put off your old self, which is being corrupted by its deceitful desires; [23] to be made new in the attitude of your minds; [24] and to put on the new self, created to be like God in true righteousness and holiness.

[25] Therefore each of you must put off falsehood and speak truthfully to your neighbor, for we are all members of one body. [26] "In your anger do not sin": Do not let the sun go down while you are still angry, [27] and do not give the devil a foothold. [28] Anyone who has been stealing must steal no longer, but must work, doing something useful with their own hands, that they may have something to share with those in need.

[29] Do not let any unwholesome talk come out of your mouths, but only what is helpful for building others up according to their needs, that it may benefit those who listen. [30] And do not grieve the Holy Spirit of God, with whom you were sealed for the day of redemption. [31] Get rid of all bitterness, rage and anger, brawling and slander, along with every form of malice. [32] Be kind and compassionate to one another, forgiving each other, just as in Christ God forgave you.

## NEW KING JAMES VERSION

[17] This I say, therefore, and testify in the Lord, that you should no longer walk as the rest of the Gentiles walk, in the futility of their mind, [18] having their understanding darkened, being alienated from the life of God, because of the ignorance that is in them, because of the blindness of their heart; [19] who, being past feeling, have given themselves over to lewdness, to work all uncleanness with greediness.

[20] But you have not so learned Christ, [21] if indeed you have heard Him and have been taught by Him, as the truth is in Jesus: [22] that you put

off, concerning your former conduct, the old man which grows corrupt according to the deceitful lusts, ²³ and be renewed in the spirit of your mind, ²⁴ and that you put on the new man which was created according to God, in true righteousness and holiness.

²⁵ Therefore, putting away lying, "Let each one of you speak truth with his neighbor," for we are members of one another. ²⁶ "Be angry, and do not sin": do not let the sun go down on your wrath, ²⁷ nor give place to the devil. ²⁸ Let him who stole steal no longer, but rather let him labor, working with his hands what is good, that he may have something to give him who has need. ²⁹ Let no corrupt word proceed out of your mouth, but what is good for necessary edification, that it may impart grace to the hearers. ³⁰ And do not grieve the Holy Spirit of God, by whom you were sealed for the day of redemption. ³¹ Let all bitterness, wrath, anger, clamor, and evil speaking be put away from you, with all malice. ³² And be kind to one another, tenderhearted, forgiving one another, even as God in Christ forgave you.

# EXPLORATION

**1.** How does Paul describe the Ephesian believers' former lives?

_____

_____

_____

_____

_____

**2.** What does Paul say they are to "put off" now that they are followers of Jesus?

_____

_____

_____

_____

_____

**3.** How would you describe the difference between the "old self" and the "new self"?

**4.** How does speaking truthfully support and build up the body of Christ? How does telling lies, gossiping, and unwholesome talk break it down?

**5.** What does Paul mean when says not to give the devil a "foothold" in your life?

**6.** What does Paul say we are to do with our words and actions?

# INSPIRATION

Insensitivity makes a wound that heals slowly. If someone hurts your feelings intentionally, you know how to react. You know the source of the pain. But if someone accidentally bruises your soul, it's difficult to know how to respond.

Someone at work criticizes the new boss who also happens to be your dear friend. "Oh, I'm sorry—I forgot the two of you were so close."

A joke is told at a party about overweight people. You're overweight. You hear the joke. You smile politely while your heart sinks.

What was intended to be a reprimand for a decision or action becomes a personal attack. "You have a history of poor decisions, John."

Someone chooses to wash your dirty laundry in public. "Sue, is it true that you and Jim are separated?"

Insensitive comments. Thoughts that should have remained thoughts. Feelings which had no business being expressed. Opinions carelessly tossed like a grenade into a crowd.

And if you were to tell the one who threw these thoughtless darts about the pain they caused, his or her response would be, "Oh, but I had no intention . . . ," or, "I didn't realize you were so sensitive," or, "I forgot you were here."

In a way, the words are comforting, until you stop to think about them (which is not recommended). For when you start to think about insensitive slurs, you realize they come from an infamous family whose father has bred generations of pain. His name? Egotism. His children? Three sisters: disregard, disrespect, and disappointment.

These three witches have combined to poison countless relationships and break innumerable hearts. Listed among their weapons are Satan's cruelest artillery: gossip, accusations, resentment, impatience, and on and on . . .

God's Word has strong medicine for those who carelessly wag their tongues. The message is clear: He who dares to call himself God's ambassador is not afforded the luxury of idle words. Excuses such as "I didn't know you were here" or "I didn't realize this was so touchy" are shallow when they come from those who claim to be followers and imitators of the Great Physician. We have an added responsibility to guard our tongues. (From *God Came Near* by Max Lucado.)

# REACTION

**7.** Why do believers in Christ often say things to hurt others—even though God clearly instructs them not to do so?

_____

_____

_____

_____

**8.** Why does it feel good at times to put others down?

_____

_____

_____

_____

**9.** How does God view your actions when you disregard or disrespect others?

_____

_____

_____

_____

**10.** Anger in and of itself is not a sin. However, what are some ways it can quickly lead to sin?

_____

_____

_____

**11.** What are some ways you have learned to redirect a conversation when a friend wants to gossip or speak badly about another person who is not present?

_____

_____

_____

_____

**12.** What are some ways that you seek to build others up with your words?

_____

_____

_____

_____

# LIFE LESSONS

The need to be aware of and alter our speech offers us one of the most obvious areas for spiritual growth. Paul lays out a "training plan" in this regard for personal transformation. Honesty with ourselves and with others becomes a foundation for other changes in life. Without personal integrity, the capacity even to acknowledge other problem areas will be severely limited. God's Word goes a long way to eliminate any guessing about areas that we need to address as we "walk worthy" of our calling (Ephesians 4:1 NKJV).

# DEVOTION

_Father, we do not have the strength within ourselves to be transformed into your likeness and not be conformed to this world. We invite your assistance today in guiding our words and our actions so they will build others up instead of tear them down. Teach us to speak with your voice and love with your love._

# JOURNALING

How does remembering the way God has been compassionate to me help me to extend the same compassion to others through my words and actions?

# FOR FURTHER READING

To complete the book of Ephesians during this twelve-part study, read Ephesians 4:17–32. For more Bible passages on speech that pleases God, read Proverbs 16:24; 25:11; Ecclesiastes 10:12; Isaiah 50:4; Ephesians 4:29; and Colossians 4:6.

# WALKING IN THE LIGHT

*You were once darkness, but now you are*
*light in the Lord. Live as children of light . . .*
*and find out what pleases the Lord.*
EPHESIANS 5:8, 10

# REFLECTION

Part of walking in God's light means being wise. Think of the wisest people you know. What are some things they do that you consider to be wise? In what ways are they similar or different from other people you know?

_____

_____

_____

_____

_____

_____

_____

_____

_____

_____

# SITUATION

The apostle Paul, having begun his instruction to the believers on what kinds of behaviors they are to "put off," continues to expand in this section on the types of actions that are not representative of walking in God's light, love, and wisdom. The analogy of "walking" is a good one for the Christian life, for it implies a continued journey with. Christians have the ability to change their behaviors along the way, but they must be willing to follow where God leads.

# OBSERVATION

*Read Ephesians 5:1–21 from the New International
Version or the New King James Version.*

## New International Version

[1] Follow God's example, therefore, as dearly loved children [2] and walk in the way of love, just as Christ loved us and gave himself up for us as a fragrant offering and sacrifice to God.

[3] But among you there must not be even a hint of sexual immorality, or of any kind of impurity, or of greed, because these are improper for God's holy people. [4] Nor should there be obscenity, foolish talk or coarse joking, which are out of place, but rather thanksgiving. [5] For of this you can be sure: No immoral, impure or greedy person—such a person is an idolater—has any inheritance in the kingdom of Christ and of God. [6] Let no one deceive you with empty words, for because of such things God's wrath comes on those who are disobedient. [7] Therefore do not be partners with them.

[8] For you were once darkness, but now you are light in the Lord. Live as children of light [9] (for the fruit of the light consists in all goodness, righteousness and truth) [10] and find out what pleases the Lord. [11] Have nothing to do with the fruitless deeds of darkness, but rather expose them. [12] It is shameful even to mention what the disobedient do in secret. [13] But everything exposed by the light becomes visible—and everything that is illuminated becomes a light. [14] This is why it is said:

> "Wake up, sleeper,
>> rise from the dead,
>> and Christ will shine on you."

[15] Be very careful, then, how you live—not as unwise but as wise, [16] making the most of every opportunity, because the days are evil. [17] Therefore do not be foolish, but understand what the Lord's will is. [18] Do not get drunk on wine, which leads to debauchery. Instead, be filled with

the Spirit, [19] speaking to one another with psalms, hymns, and songs from the Spirit. Sing and make music from your heart to the Lord, [20] always giving thanks to God the Father for everything, in the name of our Lord Jesus Christ. [21] Submit to one another out of reverence for Christ.

## NEW KING JAMES VERSION

[1] Therefore be imitators of God as dear children. [2] And walk in love, as Christ also has loved us and given Himself for us, an offering and a sacrifice to God for a sweet-smelling aroma.

[3] But fornication and all uncleanness or covetousness, let it not even be named among you, as is fitting for saints; [4] neither filthiness, nor foolish talking, nor coarse jesting, which are not fitting, but rather giving of thanks. [5] For this you know, that no fornicator, unclean person, nor covetous man, who is an idolater, has any inheritance in the kingdom of Christ and God. [6] Let no one deceive you with empty words, for because of these things the wrath of God comes upon the sons of disobedience. [7] Therefore do not be partakers with them.

[8] For you were once darkness, but now you are light in the Lord. Walk as children of light [9] (for the fruit of the Spirit is in all goodness, righteousness, and truth), [10] finding out what is acceptable to the Lord. [11] And have no fellowship with the unfruitful works of darkness, but rather expose them. [12] For it is shameful even to speak of those things which are done by them in secret. [13] But all things that are exposed are made manifest by the light, for whatever makes manifest is light. [14] Therefore He says:

> "Awake, you who sleep,
> Arise from the dead,
> And Christ will give you light."

[15] See then that you walk circumspectly, not as fools but as wise, [16] redeeming the time, because the days are evil.

[17] Therefore do not be unwise, but understand what the will of the Lord is. [18] And do not be drunk with wine, in which is dissipation; but

be filled with the Spirit, [19] speaking to one another in psalms and hymns and spiritual songs, singing and making melody in your heart to the Lord, [20] giving thanks always for all things to God the Father in the name of our Lord Jesus Christ, [21] submitting to one another in the fear of God.

# EXPLORATION

**1.** What is the difference between a life that is full of darkness and a life that is full of light?

**2.** Paul says there should be no "obscenity, foolish talk or coarse joking" among believers in Christ (verse 4). Why is it important not even joke about or make light of sin?

**3.** How would a person be deceived with "empty words" (verse 6)? Why do you think felt it necessary to add this point when addressing the Ephesian believers?

**4.** Paul instructs believers in this passage to learn what pleases God. What does this have to do with walking in love?

**5.** We probably all know some signs of being "drunk on wine" (verse 18). What are some signs of being filled with the Spirit?

_____

_____

_____

**6.** Why is it critical to give "thanks to the Father for everything" as we seek to walk in his light and follow his ways (verse 20)?

_____

_____

_____

# INSPIRATION

When you make a list of history's harshest scourges, rank the Black Plague near the top. It earns a high spot. But not the highest. Call the disease catastrophic, disastrous. But humanity's deadliest? No. Scripture reserves that title for a darker blight, an older pandemic that by comparison makes the Black Plague seem like a cold sore. No culture avoids, no nation escapes, no person sidesteps the infection of _sin_. . . .

Where we might think of sin as slip-ups or missteps, God views sin as a godless attitude that leads to godless actions. "We all, like sheep, have gone astray, each of us has turned to our own way" (Isaiah 53:6). The sinful mind dismisses God. His counsel goes unconsulted. His opinion, unsolicited. His plan, unconsidered. The sin-infected grant God the same respect middle-schoolers give a substitute teacher—acknowledged, but not taken seriously.

The lack of God-centeredness leads to self-centeredness. Sin celebrates its middle letter—sIn. It proclaims, "It's your life, right? Pump your body with drugs, your mind with greed, your nights with pleasure." The godless lead a me-dominated, childish life, a life of "doing what we felt like doing, when we felt like doing it" (Ephesians 2:3 MSG).

God says to love. I choose to hate.

God instructs, "Forgive." I opt to get even.

God calls for self-control. I promote self-indulgence.

Sin, for a season, quenches thirst. But so does salt water. Given time, the thirst returns, more demanding and demanding more than ever. "They have lost all feeling of shame, and they use their lives for doing evil. They *continually* want to do all kinds of evil" (Ephesians 4:19 NCV, emphasis mine). . . .

God has made it clear. The plague of sin will not cross his shores. Infected souls never walk his streets. God refuses to compromise the spiritual purity of heaven. . . . So what can we do? If all have been infected and the world is corrupted, to whom do we turn? Or, to re-ask the great question of Scripture: "What must I do to be saved?" (Acts 16:30). The answer offered then is the answer offered still: "Put your entire trust in the Master Jesus" (Acts 16:31 MSG). (From *Come Thirsty* by Max Lucado.)

## REACTION

**7.** What are some of the characteristics of a mind infected with sin?

_____

_____

_____

**8.** How does Paul make it clear to the Ephesian believers that God will not tolerate sin?

_____

_____

_____

**9.** How does sin quench a person's thirst—but only for a season?

_____

_____

_____

**10.** What are some of the ways that you can walk in the light?

_____

_____

_____

**11.** Why is it important to make "the most of every opportunity" when it comes to serving God and being wise (verse 15)?

_____

_____

_____

**12.** What are benefits of having a heart filled with gratitude?

_____

_____

_____

# LIFE LESSONS

The process of imitating God will affect many areas of our lives. While we cannot exactly duplicate walking in the standards of love, light, and wisdom that are part of God's holy and perfect character, we can seek to continually _imitate_ those qualities—and reap the benefits from them. As humans, we bear the image of God; as believers in Jesus, we seek to live up to his pattern. He has invited us to live that way and has promised us the help we will need. Our progress will show an increasing presence of love, light, and wisdom in our lives.

# DEVOTION

_God, you have given us clear instruction in your Word to avoid walking in the darkness of sin and to instead choose the light that you offer. Thank you for the promise and gift of salvation. Today, we ask you to forgive us_ *when we sometimes put more hope in the things of this earth than in the incredible promises of your heaven. Teach us to live in your light.*

# JOURNALING

What are some reasons why you sometimes choose darkness instead of light?

# FOR FURTHER READING

To complete the book of Ephesians during this twelve-part study, read Ephesians 5:1–21. For more Bible passages on living in the light, read John 3:19–21; Acts 26:15–18; Romans 13:11–14; 2 Corinthians 4:6; 1 Peter 2:9–10; and 1 John 1:5–10.

# DON'T MISS THE YIELD SIGNS

*Wives, submit to your own husbands, as to the Lord.... Husbands, love your wives, just as Christ also loved the church and gave Himself for her.*

EPHESIANS 5:22, 25 NKJV

# REFLECTION

Yield signs come in all shapes, sizes, and forms in our lives. When was a time that God put up a yield sign in your life for something you were pursuing? How did you react?

_____

_____

_____

_____

_____

# SITUATION

Paul has now given detailed instruction to the Ephesian believers on what it means to be one in Christ, turn from their former sinful behaviors, and learn to walk in God's light, love, and wisdom. Having laid this framework, he now reaches the heart of his practical theology by focusing on three crucial relationships that will test his readers' understanding of the concepts he has set before them. He begins in this first section by speaking about the relationship that should exist between Christian husbands and wives.

# OBSERVATION

*Read Ephesians 5:22–33 from the New International*
*Version or the New King James Version.*

NEW INTERNATIONAL VERSION

²² Wives, submit yourselves to your own husbands as you do to the Lord.
²³ For the husband is the head of the wife as Christ is the head of the

church, his body, of which he is the Savior. [24] Now as the church submits to Christ, so also wives should submit to their husbands in everything.

[25] Husbands, love your wives, just as Christ loved the church and gave himself up for her [26] to make her holy, cleansing her by the washing with water through the word, [27] and to present her to himself as a radiant church, without stain or wrinkle or any other blemish, but holy and blameless. [28] In this same way, husbands ought to love their wives as their own bodies. He who loves his wife loves himself. [29] After all, no one ever hated their own body, but they feed and care for their body, just as Christ does the church— [30] for we are members of his body. [31] "For this reason a man will leave his father and mother and be united to his wife, and the two will become one flesh." [32] This is a profound mystery—but I am talking about Christ and the church. [33] However, each one of you also must love his wife as he loves himself, and the wife must respect her husband.

## NEW KING JAMES VERSION

[22] Wives, submit to your own husbands, as to the Lord. [23] For the husband is head of the wife, as also Christ is head of the church; and He is the Savior of the body. [24] Therefore, just as the church is subject to Christ, so let the wives be to their own husbands in everything.

[25] Husbands, love your wives, just as Christ also loved the church and gave Himself for her, [26] that He might sanctify and cleanse her with the washing of water by the word, [27] that He might present her to Himself a glorious church, not having spot or wrinkle or any such thing, but that she should be holy and without blemish. [28] So husbands ought to love their own wives as their own bodies; he who loves his wife loves himself. [29] For no one ever hated his own flesh, but nourishes and cherishes it, just as the Lord does the church. [30] For we are members of His body, of His flesh and of His bones. [31] "For this reason a man shall leave his father and mother and be joined to his wife, and the two shall become one flesh." [32] This is a great mystery, but I speak concerning Christ and the church. [33] Nevertheless let each one of you in particular so love his own wife as himself, and let the wife see that she respects her husband.

# EXPLORATION

**1.** What makes it difficult to yield to someone else's wants and needs instead of your own?

_____

_____

_____

_____

_____

**2.** Is the term submit an absolutely negative term for you? When might it be positive?

_____

_____

_____

_____

_____

**3.** In this passage, Paul compares the husband's role in a marriage to Christ's role as the head of the church. What responsibilities does the husband have?

_____

_____

_____

_____

_____

**4.** How can wives honor their husbands as the church honors Christ?

_____

_____

_____

_____

_____

**5.** In what ways can husbands give their lives for their wives as Paul says they should?

_____

_____

_____

**6.** What is the relationship between love and respect in a marriage?

_____

_____

_____

# INSPIRATION

Let's talk for a minute about lovebursts. You've witnessed _sunbursts_: sunlight shafting into a shadowed forest. You've seen _starbursts_: shots of light soaring through a night sky. And you've heard _powerbursts_: raw energy booming in the silence. And you've felt _lovebursts_. You may not have called them such, but you've felt them.

Lovebursts. Spontaneous affection. Tender moments of radiant love. Ignited devotion. Explosions of tenderness. May I illustrate? . . .

Let's say you came home cranky because a deadline got moved up. She came home grumpy because the daycare forgot to give your five-year-old her throat medicine. Each of you wanted a little sympathy from the other, but neither got any. So there you sit at the dinner table—cranky and grumpy—with little Emily.

Emily folds her hands to pray (as she has been taught), and the two of you bow your heads (but not your hearts) and listen. From where this prayer comes, God only knows.

"God, it's Emily. How are you? I'm fine, thank you. Mom and Dad are mad. I don't know why. We've got birds and toys and mashed potatoes and each other. Maybe you can get them to stop being mad? Please do, or it's just gonna be you and me having any fun tonight. Amen."

The prayer is answered before it's finished. You both look up in the middle, and laugh at the end, and shake your heads and say you're sorry. And you both thank God for the little voice who reminded you about what matters. (From *He Still Moves Stones* by Max Lucado.)

# REACTION

**7.** Throughout Paul's letter, he encourages the Ephesian believers to honor and respect one another. How does this play out in situations like the one above?

_____

_____

_____

_____

**8.** What are some tactics that could help a couple regain perspective when situations get tense?

_____

_____

_____

**9.** What does it mean to truly yield or submit to someone or something?

_____

_____

_____

**10.** How does Paul say that wives are to submit to their husbands (see verse 22)? What kind of sacrifice does this require?

_____

_____

_____

**11.** How does Paul say that husbands are to love their wives (see verse 25)? What kind of sacrifice does this require?

_____

_____

_____

**12.** In what ways will respecting Christ help couples to better yield to each other?

_____

_____

_____

## LIFE LESSONS

Because a long-term relationship involves two people, it cannot be a democracy. Life presents decisions that must be made even if there is a disagreement. In a union of two, there can be harmony on most issues. But when there is a nonnegotiable disagreement, someone must have the responsibility of the deciding vote. This responsibility must be stated beforehand and affirmed in the middle of the situation. This is the essential challenge and opportunity of love and respect. The lessons God teaches are not just learned. They are learned, lived, and then learned again and again. And all the while, living goes on.

## DEVOTION

_God, give us strength as we try to be more like Jesus in our homes. Keep the evil one away from us. Keep us close to you. Let our homes be testimonies of your love for us. When people look inside, let them see how you have loved the world._

# JOURNALING

In what ways can you bend more this week to mend a relationship?

_____

_____

_____

_____

_____

_____

_____

_____

_____

_____

_____

_____

_____

_____

_____

_____

_____

_____

# FOR FURTHER READING

To complete the book of Ephesians during this twelve-part study, read Ephesians 5:22–33. For more Bible passages on marriage relationships, read Ecclesiastes 4:9–12; 1 Corinthians 7:1–7; Colossians 3:18–19; Hebrews 13:4–6; and 1 Peter 3:1–7.

# GOOD PARENTS, GOOD BOSSES

*Children, obey your parents in the Lord. . . . Fathers, do not exasperate your children. . . . Slaves, obey your earthly masters with respect and fear, and with sincerity of heart, just as you would obey Christ. . . . And masters, treat your slaves in the same way.*
EPHESIANS 6:1, 4, 5, 9

# REFLECTION

Think of a situation in which you had to submit to someone else's authority—whether that was a parent when you were young, or a boss when you were older. Why is it often so hard to submit to those in authority? Why is it necessary to do so?

_____

_____

_____

_____

_____

_____

_____

_____

_____

_____

# SITUATION

Paul now focuses on two other types of relationships in which believers in Christ are to live out the godly principles he has outlined: children and parents, and slaves and masters. Women in Paul's day had few rights, and children and slaves had practically none at all. So, when Paul addressed these persons as individuals capable of privileges, responsibilities, and expectations, he was significantly elevating their status in society. He was giving them worth by addressing them and importance by requiring others in the body of Christ to treat them with respect.

# OBSERVATION

*Read Ephesians 6:1–9 from the New International*
*Version or the New King James Version.*

## New International Version

[1] Children, obey your parents in the Lord, for this is right. [2] "Honor your father and mother"—which is the first commandment with a promise— [3] "so that it may go well with you and that you may enjoy long life on the earth."

[4] Fathers, do not exasperate your children; instead, bring them up in the training and instruction of the Lord.

[5] Slaves, obey your earthly masters with respect and fear, and with sincerity of heart, just as you would obey Christ. [6] Obey them not only to win their favor when their eye is on you, but as slaves of Christ, doing the will of God from your heart. [7] Serve wholeheartedly, as if you were serving the Lord, not people, [8] because you know that the Lord will reward each one for whatever good they do, whether they are slave or free.

[9] And masters, treat your slaves in the same way. Do not threaten them, since you know that he who is both their Master and yours is in heaven, and there is no favoritism with him.

## New King James Version

[1] Children, obey your parents in the Lord, for this is right. [2] "Honor your father and mother," which is the first commandment with promise: [3] "that it may be well with you and you may live long on the earth."

[4] And you, fathers, do not provoke your children to wrath, but bring them up in the training and admonition of the Lord.

[5] Bondservants, be obedient to those who are your masters according to the flesh, with fear and trembling, in sincerity of heart, as to Christ; [6] not with eyeservice, as men-pleasers, but as bondservants of Christ, doing the will of God from the heart, [7] with goodwill doing service, as to

the Lord, and not to men, [8] knowing that whatever good anyone does, he will receive the same from the Lord, whether he is a slave or free.

[9] And you, masters, do the same things to them, giving up threatening, knowing that your own Master also is in heaven, and there is no partiality with Him.

# EXPLORATION

**1.** God's standard is that children are to obey their parents in keeping with their commitment to follow Christ. How would you describe this kind of obedience?

_____

_____

_____

**2.** What are some of the benefits of children obeying their parents (see Deuteronomy 5:16)?

_____ _long life & happy home_ _____

_____

_____

**3.** How can dads keep from making their children angry? How does this relate to the fact that kids often get upset when they are corrected or disciplined?

_____

_____

_____

**4.** In what ways do Paul's instructions to slaves (to work with integrity whether the master is watching or not) apply to employees?

_____

_____

_____

**5.** Paul reminds masters that they and their slaves are both serving the same master (God). In what ways does this truth apply to bosses or managers?

_____

_____

_____

**6.** Why would the Bible say to do your work with enthusiasm?

_____

_____

_____

# INSPIRATION

What does it mean to honor your parents? We can see what it means if we will look at the word _honor_ in the Scriptures. In Hebrew, the word for "honor" is _kabed_. This word literally means, "to be heavy, weighty, to honor." Even today, we still link the idea of being heavy with honoring a person.

When the President of the United States or some other important person speaks, people often say that his words "carry a lot of weight." Someone whose words are weighty is someone worthy of honor and respect. However, we can learn even more about what it means to honor someone by looking at its opposite in Scriptures . . .

The literal meaning of the word "curse" _(qalal)_ was "to make light, of little weight, to dishonor." If we go back to our example above, if we dishonor a person we would say, "Their words carry little weight." The contrast is striking!

When Paul tells us to honor our parents, he is telling us that they are worthy of high value and respect. In modern-day terms, we could call them a heavyweight in our lives! Just the opposite is true if we choose to dishonor our parents.

Some people treat their parents as if they are a layer of dust on a table. Dust weighs almost nothing and can be swept away with a brush of the hand. Dust is a nuisance and an eyesore that clouds any real beauty the table might have. Paul tells us that such an attitude should not be a part of how any child views his or her parents and for good reason. If we fail to honor our parents, we not only do what is wrong and dishonor God, but we also literally drain ourselves of life! (From *The Gift of the Blessing* by Gary Smalley and John Trent.)

## REACTION

**7.** In what ways can you honor your parents? What does it mean to honor your parents as a college student? Or as a newly married couple?

_____

_____

_____

_____

**8.** What makes honoring your parents difficult in your life?

_____

_____

_____

_____

**9.** Is disregarding your parents the same as dishonoring them? Why or why not?

_____

_____

_____

_____

**10.** In what way is God honored by your diligent work in your job?

 

 

**11.** How do you think God will reward everyone for doing good?

 

 

**12.** What is the proper way to handle a problem you might have with a person in authority—whether that is a parent, employee, or anyone else?

 

 

## LIFE LESSONS

The challenge in relationships comes in part because they are two-sided arrangements. Paul's words in this passage looks at both sides—children and parents, and workers and bosses. Spiritual maturity comes when we can see the side other than our own. A sense of our needs, desires, and rights comes naturally, while an appreciation for others' needs, desires, and rights comes not-so-naturally. And beyond, the willingness to act on what we understand of someone else's position depends heavily on God's help.

## DEVOTION

*Lift up our eyes, Father, that we might see ourselves and those around us as you see us. Help us to respond to one another with love and compassion. Help us to be like you.*

# JOURNALING

What can you do this week to show honor to your parents or to your employer?

_____

_____

_____

_____

_____

_____

_____

_____

_____

_____

_____

_____

_____

_____

_____

# FOR FURTHER READING

To complete the book of Ephesians during this twelve-part study, read Ephesians 6:1–9. For more Bible passages on the relationships discussed in this lesson, read Matthew 25:14–30; Colossians 3:20–25; 1 Timothy 3:2–5; 6:1–2; Titus 2:3–5; and 1 Peter 2:18–25.

# LESSON TWELVE

# ARMOR UP

*Put on the whole armor of God, that you may be
able to stand against the wiles of the devil.*
EPHESIANS 6:11 NKJV

# REFLECTION

Think of a time when you were involved in a victory of some kind. What preparation was needed to get there? What are the feelings that come from being on the winning side?

_____

_____

_____

_____

# SITUATION

Paul began his letter by talking about the riches, privileges, and benefits that all believers have been given in Christ (see Ephesians 1–3). He went on to explain the believers' role in pursuing a godly life worthy of this calling (see Ephesians 4–6:9). He now concludes by using a metaphor to remind his readers that a very real battle is being waged for their souls. By equipping the "armor" that God has given them for this fight, they can be prepared for the onslaught of the enemy and ready for the life of adventure the Lord has for them in his service.

# OBSERVATION

*Read Ephesians 6:10–24 from the New International*
*Version or the New King James Version.*

New International Version

[10] Finally, be strong in the Lord and in his mighty power. [11] Put on the full armor of God, so that you can take your stand against the devil's schemes. [12] For our struggle is not against flesh and blood, but against the rulers, against the authorities, against the powers of this dark world and

against the spiritual forces of evil in the heavenly realms. [13] Therefore put on the full armor of God, so that when the day of evil comes, you may be able to stand your ground, and after you have done everything, to stand. [14] Stand firm then, with the belt of truth buckled around your waist, with the breastplate of righteousness in place, [15] and with your feet fitted with the readiness that comes from the gospel of peace. [16] In addition to all this, take up the shield of faith, with which you can extinguish all the flaming arrows of the evil one. [17] Take the helmet of salvation and the sword of the Spirit, which is the word of God.

[18] And pray in the Spirit on all occasions with all kinds of prayers and requests. With this in mind, be alert and always keep on praying for all the Lord's people. [19] Pray also for me, that whenever I speak, words may be given me so that I will fearlessly make known the mystery of the gospel, [20] for which I am an ambassador in chains. Pray that I may declare it fearlessly, as I should.

[21] Tychicus, the dear brother and faithful servant in the Lord, will tell you everything, so that you also may know how I am and what I am doing. [22] I am sending him to you for this very purpose, that you may know how we are, and that he may encourage you.

[23] Peace to the brothers and sisters, and love with faith from God the Father and the Lord Jesus Christ. [24] Grace to all who love our Lord Jesus Christ with an undying love.

## New King James Version

[10] Finally, my brethren, be strong in the Lord and in the power of His might. [11] Put on the whole armor of God, that you may be able to stand against the wiles of the devil. [12] For we do not wrestle against flesh and blood, but against principalities, against powers, against the rulers of the darkness of this age, against spiritual hosts of wickedness in the heavenly places. [13] Therefore take up the whole armor of God, that you may be able to withstand in the evil day, and having done all, to stand.

[14] Stand therefore, having girded your waist with truth, having put on the breastplate of righteousness, [15] and having shod your feet with the

preparation of the gospel of peace; [16] above all, taking the shield of faith with which you will be able to quench all the fiery darts of the wicked one. [17] And take the helmet of salvation, and the sword of the Spirit, which is the word of God; [18] praying always with all prayer and supplication in the Spirit, being watchful to this end with all perseverance and supplication for all the saints— [19] and for me, that utterance may be given to me, that I may open my mouth boldly to make known the mystery of the gospel, [20] for which I am an ambassador in chains; that in it I may speak boldly, as I ought to speak.

[21] But that you also may know my affairs and how I am doing, Tychicus, a beloved brother and faithful minister in the Lord, will make all things known to you; [22] whom I have sent to you for this very purpose, that you may know our affairs, and that he may comfort your hearts.

[23] Peace to the brethren, and love with faith, from God the Father and the Lord Jesus Christ. [24] Grace be with all those who love our Lord Jesus Christ in sincerity. Amen.

# EXPLORATION

**1.** What is the purpose of a soldier's armor? Why does Paul advise Christians to equip the "full armor of God" (verse 11)?

_____

_____

_____

_____

**2.** How does Paul describe a believer's struggle to live for Christ? What kind of "schemes" might the enemy use to try to knock you off course?

_____

_____

_____

**3.** What does it mean to "stand your ground" in the battles you face?

_____

_____

_____

**4.** In what ways will a life of prayer benefit you in spiritual warfare?

_____

_____

_____

**5.** Why is it important to pray "on all occasions" and "keep on praying" when facing the enemy (verse 18; see also Luke 18:1–8)?

_____

_____

_____

_____

**6.** What is Paul's closing request to the Ephesian believers? What does this request tell you about what he felt his priorities and purpose were on this earth?

_____

_____

## INSPIRATION

Triumph is a precious thing. We honor the triumphant. The gallant soldier sitting astride his steed. The determined explorer returning from his discovery. The winning athlete holding aloft the triumphant trophy of victory. Yes, we love triumph.

Triumph brings with it a swell of purpose and meaning. When I'm triumphant, I'm worthy. When I'm triumphant, I count. When I'm triumphant, I'm significant.

Triumph is fleeting, though. Hardly does one taste victory before it is gone; achieved, yet now history. No one remains champion forever. Time for yet another conquest, another victory. Perhaps this is the absurdity of Paul's claim: "But thanks be to God, who always leads us as captives in Christ's triumphal procession" (2 Corinthians 2:14).

The triumph of Christ is not temporary. "Triumphant in Christ" is not an event or an occasion. It's not fleeting. To be triumphant in Christ is a lifestyle . . . a state of being! To triumph in Christ is not something we do; it's something we are.

Here is the big difference between victory in Christ and victory in the world. A victor in the world rejoices over something he did—swimming the English Channel, climbing Mount Everest, making a million. But the believer rejoices over who he is: a child of God, a forgiven sinner, an heir of eternity. As the hymn goes, "Heir of salvation, purchase of God, born of his Spirit, washed in his blood."

Nothing can separate us from our triumph in Christ. Nothing! Our triumph is not based upon our feelings but upon God's gift. Our triumph is based not upon our perfection but upon God's forgiveness. How precious is this triumph! For even though we are pressed on every side, the victory is still ours. Nothing can alter the loyalty of God.

A friend of mine once lost his father to death. The faith of his father had for years served as an inspiration for many. In moments alone with the body of his father, my friend said this thought kept coming to his mind as he looked at his daddy's face: "You won. You won. You won!" As Joan of Arc said when she was abandoned by those who should have stood by her, "It is better to be alone with God. His friendship will not fail me, nor his counsel, nor his love. In his strength I will dare and dare and dare until I die."

"Triumphant in Christ." It is not something we do. It's something we are. (From *Shaped by God* by Max Lucado.)

# REACTION

**7.** In what ways are Christians like soldiers seeking triumph over an enemy?

**8.** How would you define "spiritual victory"?

**9.** How can truth, righteousness, and peace help you to stand against the enemy's attacks?

**10.** In what way is faith like a shield? How is salvation like a helmet?

**11.** In what way is the Word of God like a sword? What would it take for you to feel comfortable going into battle with this "sword"?

_____

_____

_____

**12.** What degree of battle readiness would you give yourself? What can you do to each day better equip the armor that God has given to you?

_____

_____

_____

# LIFE LESSONS

God does all the crucial work and provides all the essential resources. He challenges and encourages us to use them. Each item of spiritual armor listed in this passage comes to us as a gift from God, and he guarantees their effectiveness. But their effectiveness is limited by our willingness to "put them on" and use them. Along with walking by faith, walking worthy, walking in light, and walking in love, there are also times for standing firm. Life situations may involve taking a stand—and when we do, it's best not to do so unarmed. With faith, truth, salvation, the Word of God, and prayer, God has promised us victory.

# DEVOTION

_Lord, we give you all praise today. We honor and glorify your name. You truly are the King of Kings and the Lord of Lords! Thank you for equipping us for victory against the enemy. Help us to take up the armor you have provided and battle our enemy with the weapon of your Word. May we worship you always and give you the credit for every victory we achieve. Amen._

# JOURNALING

What are some areas in your life where you need God's armor to help you stand firm?

_____

_____

_____

_____

_____

_____

_____

_____

_____

_____

_____

_____

_____

_____

_____

_____

_____

_____

_____

_____

_____

_____

_____

_____

_____

# FOR FURTHER READING

To complete the book of Ephesians during this twelve-part study, read Ephesians 6:10–24. For more Bible passages on victory in Christ, read Psalm 44:4–8; 60:12; 118:13–16; Proverbs 2:6–8; 21:30–31; 1 Corinthians 15:54–57; and 1 John 5:3–5.

# LEADER'S GUIDE FOR SMALL GROUPS

Thank you for your willingness to lead a group through *Life Lessons from Ephesians*. The rewards of being a leader are different from those of participating, and we hope you find your own walk with Jesus deepened by this experience. During the twelve lessons in this study, you will guide your group through selected passages in Ephesians and explore the key themes of the letter. There are several elements in this leader's guide that will help you as you structure your study and reflection time, so be sure to follow along and take advantage of each one.

## BEFORE YOU BEGIN

Before your first meeting, make sure the group members have their own copy of the *Life Lessons from Ephesians* study guide so they can follow along and have their answers written out ahead of time. Alternately, you can hand out the guides at your first meeting and give the group some time to look over the material and ask any preliminary questions. Be sure to send a sheet around the room during that first meeting and have the members write down their name, phone number, and email address so you can keep in touch with them during the week.

There are two ways to structure the duration of the study. You can choose to cover each lesson individually for a total of twelve weeks of discussion, or you can combine two lessons together per week for a total of six weeks of discussion. (Note that if the group members read the selected passages of Scripture for each lesson, they will cover the entire books of Ephesians during the study.) The following table illustrates these options:

**Twelve-Week Format**

| Week | Lessons Covered | Reading |
|------|-----------------|---------|
| 1 | Where Do You Belong? | Ephesians 1:1–14 |
| 2 | The Power of Your Faith | Ephesians 1:15–23 |
| 3 | Have Mercy! | Ephesians 2:1–10 |
| 4 | Family Ties and Racial Blurs | Ephesians 2:11–22 |
| 5 | God Had a Secret? | Ephesians 3:1–13 |
| 6 | The Amazing Love of Christ | Ephesians 3:14–21 |
| 7 | Body Parts Everywhere | Ephesians 4:1–16 |
| 8 | The Power of Words | Ephesians 4:17–32 |
| 9 | Walking in the Light | Ephesians 5:1–21 |
| 10 | Don't Miss the Yield Signs | Ephesians 5:22–33 |
| 11 | Good Parents, Good Bosses | Ephesians 6:1–9 |
| 12 | Armor Up | Ephesians 6:10–24 |

**Six-Week Format**

| Week | Lessons Covered | Reading |
|------|-----------------|---------|
| 1 | Where Do You Belong? / The Power of Your Faith | Ephesians 1:1–23 |
| 2 | Have Mercy! / Family Ties and Racial Blurs | Ephesians 2:1–22 |
| 3 | God Had a Secret? / The Amazing Love of Christ | Ephesians 3:1–21 |
| 4 | Body Parts Everywhere / The Power of Words | Ephesians 4:1–32 |
| 5 | Walking in the Light / Don't Miss the Yield Signs | Ephesians 5:1–33 |
| 6 | Good Parents, Good Bosses / Armor Up | Ephesians 6:1–24 |

Generally, the ideal size you will want for the group is between eight to ten people, which ensures everyone will have enough time to participate in discussions. If you have more people, you might want to break up the main group into smaller subgroups. Encourage those who show up at the first meeting to commit to attending the duration of the study, as this will help the group members get to know each other, create stability for the group, and help you know how to prepare each week.

Each of the lessons begins with a brief reflection that highlights the theme you will be discussing that week. As you begin your group time, have the group members briefly respond to the opening question to get them thinking about the topic at hand. Some people may want to tell a long story in response to one of these questions, but the goal is to keep the answers brief. Ideally, you want everyone in the group to get a chance to answer, so try to keep the responses to just a few minutes. If you have more talkative group members, say up front that everyone needs to limit his or her answer to two minutes.

Give the group members a chance to answer, but tell them to feel free to pass if they wish. With the rest of the study, it's generally not a good idea to have everyone answer every question—a free-flowing discussion is more desirable. But with the opening reflection question, you can go around the circle. Encourage shy people to share, but don't force them.

Before your first meeting, let the group members know how the lessons are broken down. During your group discussion time the members will be drawing on the answers they wrote to the Exploration and Reaction sections, so encourage them to always complete these ahead of time. Also, invite them to bring any questions and insights they uncovered while reading to your next meeting, especially if they had a breakthrough moment or if they didn't understand something they read.

# WEEKLY PREPARATION

As the leader, there are a few things you should do to prepare for each meeting:

- *Read through the lesson.* This will help you to become familiar with the content and know how to structure the discussion times.
- *Decide which questions you want to discuss.* Depending on how you structure your group time, you may not be able to cover every

question. So select the questions ahead of time that you absolutely want the group to explore.

- *Be familiar with the questions you want to discuss.* When the group meets you'll be watching the clock, so you want to make sure you are familiar with the Bible study questions you have selected. You can then spend time in the passage again when the group meets. In this way, you'll ensure you have the passage more deeply in your mind than your group members.

- *Pray for your group.* Pray for your group members throughout the week and ask God to lead them as they study his Word.

- *Bring extra supplies to your meeting.* The members should bring their own pens for writing notes, but it's a good idea to have extras available for those who forget. You may also want to bring paper and additional Bibles.

Note that in many cases there will not be one "right" answer to the question. Answers will vary, especially when the group members are being asked to share their personal experiences.

## STRUCTURING THE DISCUSSION TIME

You will need to determine with your group how long you want to meet each week so you can plan your time accordingly. Generally, most groups like to meet for either sixty minutes or ninety minutes, so you could use one of the following schedules:

| Section | 60 Minutes | 90 Minutes |
|---|---|---|
| WELCOME (members arrive and get settled) | 5 minutes | 10 minutes |
| REFLECTION (discuss the opening question for the lesson) | 10 minutes | 15 minutes |
| DISCUSSION (discuss the Bible study questions in the Exploration and Reaction sections) | 35 minutes | 50 minutes |
| PRAYER/CLOSING (pray together as a group and dismiss) | 10 minutes | 15 minutes |

As the group leader, it is up to you to keep track of the time and keep things moving along according to your schedule. You might want to set a timer for each segment so both you and the group members know when your time is up. (Note that there are some good phone apps for timers that play a gentle chime or other pleasant sound instead of a disruptive noise.) Don't feel pressured to cover every question you have selected if the group has a good discussion going. Again, it's not necessary to go around the circle and make everyone share.

Don't be concerned if the group members are silent or slow to share. People are often quiet when they are pulling together their ideas, and this might be a new experience for them. Just ask a question and let it hang in the air until someone shares. You can then say, "Thank you. What about others? What came to you when you reflected on the passage?"

## GROUP DYNAMICS

Leading a group through *Life Lessons from Ephesians* will prove to be highly rewarding both to you and your group members—but that doesn't mean you will not encounter any challenges along the way! Discussions can get off track. Group members may not be sensitive to the needs and ideas of others. Some might worry they will be expected to talk about matters that make them feel awkward. Others may express comments that result in disagreements. To help ease this strain on you and the group, consider the following ground rules:

- When someone raises a question or comment that is off the main topic, suggest you deal with it another time, or, if you feel led to go in that direction, let the group know you will be spending some time discussing it.
- If someone asks a question you don't know how to answer, admit it and move on. At your discretion, feel free to invite group members to comment on questions that call for personal experience.

113

- If you find one or two people are dominating the discussion time, direct a few questions to others in the group. Outside the main group time, ask the more dominating members to help you draw out the quieter ones. Work to make them a part of the solution instead of the problem.
- When a disagreement occurs, encourage the group members to process the matter in love. Encourage those on opposite sides to restate what they heard the other side say about the matter, and then invite each side to evaluate if that perception is accurate. Lead the group in examining other Scriptures related to the topic and look for common ground.

When any of these issues arise, encourage your group members to follow the words from the Bible: "Love one another" (John 13:34), "If it is possible, as far as it depends on you, live at peace with everyone" (Romans 12:18), and, "Be quick to listen, slow to speak and slow to become angry" (James 1:19).

Thank you again for taking the time to lead your group. May God reward your efforts and dedication and make your time together in this study fruitful for his kingdom.

# ALSO AVAILABLE IN THE
# LIFE LESSONS SERIES

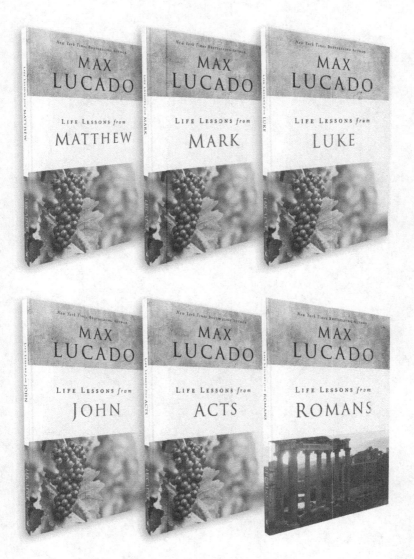

*Now available wherever books
and ebooks are sold.*